A BOWLE[illegible]
A History of Flitwick Cricket Club

John Butler, Mick Hardy, Dave Moules,
Nigel Washington and Richard Wigfield

Edited by Richard Wigfield

L to R: John Butler, Dave Moules, Mick Hardy, Richard Wigfield, Nigel Washington

First published in Great Britain by
Sitting Duck Press
2 The Avenue
Flitwick
Bedfordshire MK45 1BP

ISBN 978-0-9575823-2-3
A catalogue for this book is available from the British Library

Book & Cover Design: Sitting Duck [www.sitting-duck.org.uk]
Cover photo: Courtesy of Chris Howard-Cramer
Printed in the UK by Imprint Digital

FOREWORD

Intense rivalry, together with great mutual respect, exists between the three local Cricket Clubs at Ampthill, Eversholt and Flitwick. It is a privilege for me, as an Eversholt man, to have been asked to write the foreword to this book.

My recollections of the Flitwick Cricket Club go back more than fifty years to a time when all club cricket locally was played on a 'friendly' basis on Saturdays only and Flitwick played their home matches on the Recreation ground. Facilities were minimal, few players had their own kit and one club bag did for everyone. Balls were often used over several matches. Nevertheless competition was strong and cricket skills on display were of a high calibre.

Since then Club Cricket and how it is played have undergone massive changes. In came competitive leagues, limited overs matches, bowling restrictions, batting and bowling points and most recently power plays and free hits! Two new balls per match are mandatory and time itself only applies when a limit is placed on the length of the first innings.

Other major changes include Sunday cricket and the need for clubs to play a major role in the development of young players. Health and safety measures are an integral part of running a club. Qualified coaches have had to be trained and much time committed by them and other club members to these activities to say nothing of the compulsory CRB checks! In Bedfordshire Flitwick Cricket Club has been at the forefront in taking on these challenges.

This book commemorates the thirtieth anniversary of the opening of the current ground at The Vale. This ground epitomises the strength which the club has in coping with all situations. There is a core of highly committed members within the club devoted to maintaining its established high standards both on and off the field of play. To this group and others involved must go the credit for developing, from a green field site, the ground and associated facilities which we now know as the Flitwick Cricket Club. Regular host to County and representative fixtures and venue for numerous meetings linked to cricket administration, the club has an excellent record of service to cricket in the widest sense.

To mention names here would be invidious but the authors of the various articles are all part of that special group which has driven the club forward and continues to do so. This is indeed a proud record but it is not all. We hear today many references to 'The Spirit of Cricket' and this flourishes here at Flitwick. Visiting teams receive a warm welcome, matches are contested fiercely but fairly, and at the end of the game, whatever the result, there is always a handshake and drinks in a friendly atmosphere in the bar. It is this which makes a club great and long may it continue to do so at Flitwick.

Peter Garratt

CONTENTS

"Nearly every organisation – and ours is no exception – contains bones. 3 kinds. Wishbones, jawbones and backbones. The wishbones spend all their time wishing somebody will do the work, the jawbones are those who do all the talking, but little else and the backbones are the ones who get on and do all the work. The reason why our club has achieved so many of its objectives over its history is because we have only had a few wishbones, only 1 or 2 jawbones, but we have a lot of backbones".

Taken from the minutes of the 1981 AGM

INTRODUCTION

Records of cricket having been played in England go back a long way, and the game has provided entertainment and excitement for countless numbers. Away from the top levels, the vast majority of cricket that is played is weekend, recreational cricket, which is the starting place for many a talented cricketer who has gone on to make a name as a professional in the higher echelons of the game.

I have been very fortunate to have been associated with Flitwick Cricket Club since the early 1980s and fully intend to be for many years to come. However, it was one of the club's overseas players who prompted this piece of work, when he quite rightly noted that although there were large numbers of young players in the youth section, they only knew the pleasure of enjoying the superb facilities at The Vale. They knew nothing of the history of the club and probably just assume that it has always been there in its current format.

The club used to play opposite The Swan public house, where once could be heard the sound of leather on willow and an occasional polite 'Howzat?' enquiry to an umpire, with none of the pleading histrionics often seen in the modern game. This green area was the cricket ground but how times change. Now you will fill up with fuel somewhere near the centre of the original square. The hedges that run along the edge of the main road and by the side of the village hall which used to mark the boundary of the field are now all that remain of the original ground.

The history of clubs like ours is important and if we do not take the time to record events in some way, a little bit of local history will be lost for ever and I'm sorry, but that simply will not do. The purpose of this book therefore, is to document the story of Flitwick Cricket Club, with the aim of providing a short chronicle of how things have changed since the early days.

With any project such as this, there comes a time when one has to decide at which date we want to end. Clearly, ground improvements continue all the time, but it was felt that perhaps the 30th Anniversary of the club playing at The Vale would be an appropriate moment. I would also like to make comment regarding the photographs included. There are no doubt hundreds that have been taken over the years and selecting items such as team photographs has proved to be challenging. After all, there have been many, many such pictures taken of teams and the decision was made to include team photographs that include club members who have played a significant part in the development of the club.

Mention must be made, however, of the other club members who have turned out for the club and my sincere hope is that people will be able to associate with the photographs included in some way; be it a family association, a playing association or a friendship.

There are hundreds of cricket clubs throughout the country providing the opportunity for individuals to start on their cricket journey. Flitwick Cricket Club is one such club and this is a record of some of its history. Readers of this book who play at other clubs may well recognise a lot of similarities between the goings on at Flitwick and those of their own clubs.

I hope that this record provides memories for some, entertainment for others, and encouragement for all to ensure that the club continues to thrive and grow.

Richard Wigfield, Editor

Postscript. During the compilation of this book, the ground was officially renamed The Hardy Vale in recognition of the work and dedication of Mick Hardy. It was felt, however, that for the records of earlier times, the ground would still be referred to as The Vale.

EARLY DAYS

With a population now of around 14,000, new shops, a skateboard park, a railway line that allows access to London within 45 minutes and many other changes, Flitwick is a long way from the 10 households of 3 villagers and 7 smallholders described in the Domesday Book[1].

The origins of cricket as played in Flitwick are hidden in the mists of time. Who first suggested a game of cricket? Who first smote a ball a goodly distance and who had to retrieve it afterwards? Who lobbed the ball that it might be struck? And were they happy doing it? What was that ball made of?

We shall never know but we can imagine and smile that this was when cricket first emerged as a sport in Flitwick. Club members have gathered snippets of information from various sources, including parish magazines and county records, and these give us an idea that, when cricket first began in villages around 1790, Flitwick was at the forefront by forming a team for friendly competition.

Records of cricket in Flitwick have been traced back to 1867 and on one of the walls of the club there is a scorecard recording a match between the gentlemen of Flitwick and the gentlemen of Pulloxhill, with a newspaper cutting reporting the match dated Wednesday 11th September 1867. A win for Flitwick is reported alongside a number of local news items, giving a short glimpse of what life was like in this part of Bedfordshire at that time.

These early games, featuring no doubt the local blacksmith, schoolteacher and vicar possibly, are likely to have been played in a field called 'The Stockings', which was situated to the west of Templefield School, to the north of where Flitwick Lower School is now and to the east of the Parish Church.

1 http://domesdaymap.co.uk/place/TL0334/flitwick/

The photostat columns adjoining are from the Bedfordshire Mercury dated 24th September 1867, the original copy of which is in the Record Office, County Hall, Bedford.

There is an account of Flitwick v. Ingrith in the issue of the paper dated 20th May 1882.

In addition to the details of the match, the remainder of the column gives a good insight of the social conditions prevailing in villages at the time.

Flitwick v. Pulloxhill played on Wed. 11th September 1867

It was not until towards the end of the nineteenth century that two of the cricketers, Messrs. Baker and Pearce approached Major Brooks of Flitwick Manor, to see what could be done about a better ground. The Major provided three acres as a recreation ground by the station bridge. This was managed for some time by a committee and eventually passed to the control of the Parish Council who held ultimate responsibility for its upkeep until 1980.

The newly acquired Recreation Ground was opened by Lord Charles Russell from the Woburn Estate on 15th July 1889. This shows the feudal influence present in villages in those days. Stipulation was made that the ground should not be used inappropriately in activities such as carpet beating, for example! But the outfield was long, only being cut just before Feast day at the end of June and there were grazing rights, although these were restricted to sheep from 1906.

Although there were fixtures against local village teams it is the games played on the Flitwick Feast Day and between the veterans which figure most notably in village magazines. To play in the veterans' game, gentlemen had to be over 60 years of age. Mr Baker is reported to have played whilst still in his 80s. These matches continued well into the twentieth century. Bowling was by underarm only and batsmen had to retire on reaching 25. The umpires frequently came in for harsh criticism apparently, so although the game has developed over the years, some things never change.

Where it all really started though is somewhat uncertain, although there is an entry in the Flitwick Parish magazine dated Tuesday 16th May 1904 where a meeting was held in the Iron Room (now the site of the current Scout Hut) 'to consider if possible starting a cricket club'. Club officers were recorded as being elected, including the chairman Mr E Phillips (also elected as captain), with the comments 'we see no reason why a club under such management and with the unselfish loyalty of the members should not prove a success and win back the reputation that Flitwick Cricket used to enjoy in the days of long ago. Various matches will shortly be arranged. Members' subscription, 2/6'. That's 12.5p in today's money!

In 1897 Major Brooks was the president and Reverend Lipscomb was the chairman, showing how intricately the cricket club was part of village life as a whole. Also at the meeting were Walter Feazey, the butcher and Will Carr, the blacksmith. It would be a real challenge for even the most rural of cricket clubs to be able to field a team containing players with such occupations today.

The Parish magazine of 1905 included a report on the AGM of that year where a proposal was made to reduce the annual subscription to 2/- (that's two shillings to our younger readers!). This report also noted a working balance from the previous year of £2.13s 1d.

On 13th March 1906, the annual meeting was held in the Iron Room, with Mr Phillips in the chair. The secretary, Mr Hawtin, reported that as to cash, there was in hand from last year, £1 9s 1d. A grant from the Recreation ground

Committee towards relaying the pitch was £1 10s 0d and there were proceeds of £3 1s 0d from a concert. Against this total there had to be placed £3 4s 3d spent on the ground and printing bills. At this meeting a proposal was carried that the subscription should be reduced from 2/6d to the small sum of 2/- for the season. The secretary reported: 'We can only hope that a sufficiently large number of members who feel that they could not afford the extra 6d will be added to the roll to make up the deficiency'.

Both the magazines of 1904 and 1905 show records of matches being played against local opposition. It is probably safe to say that this was the first formal record of cricket being played under the auspices of Flitwick Cricket Club.

That season commenced on Easter Monday and Wednesday and Friday evenings were assigned practice nights.

Matches that season were not high scoring. Maulden stumbled to 29 in reply to Flitwick's 37 and the match against Ampthill at Flitwick on 15th May was a two innings affair with Flitwick mustering 35 and 55 for 6. So much for relaying the pitch! Thanks to Reverend Hunter's 33, 78 was scored against Westoning, who scored 59 in reply. The low scores recorded in these games were possibly also a testament to the poor state of the facilities in those days. The 1906 season was brought to a close with a Married v Single match on 19th September which was followed by a supper at the Swan.

Despite the onset of the first world war, there was still a desire for cricket to be played in the area. In 1914 a meeting was held in The Iron Room to start a new cricket club, efforts to restart the old club having proved unsuccessful. The meeting was 'well attended and meant business.' Mr Thomas Strickland, the Headmaster of Flitwick County Primary School seems to have been the prime mover. The report in the parish magazine testifies to his commitment.

'Mr Strickland, who has taken so much trouble in the matter already, and who, we may safely prophesy, is prepared to do a great deal more to make our village cricket club a success, will be very glad to receive subscriptions, large or small, also the names of new members ... all these payments are so arranged as to fall heavily on no one who is a lover of the old game and wishes to join. We regret that owing to the delay in starting a club this year several of our old and best players have gone elsewhere.'

Thomas Inger Strickland (Tommy) was a Yorkshireman and he took control of the school in Flitwick one year before the start of World War One. He was an enthusiastic sportsman and his organising ability was a great asset to the parish. He was a strict disciplinarian but scrupulously fair. Before coming to Flitwick he taught at Westoning School and Howard Gazeley, who was to become a prominent member of the club, said that Tommy Strickland soon sorted his class out, on arrival!

It is reported on good authority that Tommy Strickland once bowled throughout an innings in a raincoat. Weather did not deter them in those days although the current 'Loo Seat' game referred to later in this book has seen some players taking to the field with umbrellas, overcoats and gloves. 1914 would be the last year that cricket would be played until 1920, because of the war.

Richard (Dick) Dillingham, a man known by many of the senior members of the club, was born in 1914 and in his life he devoted much energy to sport. His contribution to the various sporting clubs in Ampthill is recognised in the Dillingham Park and the Richard Dillingham Pavilion. His interest in local history has contributed greatly to our understanding of who was playing after the war and beyond. The 1921 photographs stirred memories in Dick Dillingham

'I was 7 at the time of this photograph and would have seen that very team play. I knew all of them as we watched all the home games, there being no television and very few had radios or wirelesses as it was called then. So cricket and football were well supported. Howard Gazeley, George Gazeley and Bert Deacon who were playing then were still playing up to the outbreak of World War Two and Howard played beyond then. Howard's achievements are still fresh in the memory as a player, captain and organiser. His brother George was a quickish bowler and I was in the side when Bert Deacon scored over 80 against Kettering.'

'As will be noted from the low scores listed on the website, most clubs had a cricket pitch over which football was played in the winter or over which cattle and horses roamed for pasture. Selective weed killing and finer points of wicket preparation were virtually unknown, so it was not surprising that some amazing bowling figures were returned.'

Back Row, left to right: Tom Hawtin, Dave Roberts, Fred Martin, Robert Gaylor, Tommy Strickland, George Gazeley, Spot Goddard
Middle Row, left to right: Alec Goddard, Rowland Carr, Harold Gaylor, Howard Gazeley, Horace Hobbs
Front Row, left to right: Frank Gaylor, Bert Deacon, Charles Crisp

The Rec – view to the railway bridge and The Swan public house with roller that was used to prepare pitches, and as a wicket in countless summer games by youngsters

HOWARD GAZELEY AND THE RAMBLERS

Howard Gazeley is a man who remembered fondly the first motor car driving through Westoning to Flitwick, at the beginning of the twentieth century. Howard lived to be well into his nineties and for most of that time he was fanatical about cricket. Past his 65th birthday he was still scoring runs for Steppingley Cricket Club. But it was his influence on Flitwick Cricket Club which should not be undervalued.

Howard Gazeley realised that a good pitch could never be achieved on the Recreation Ground while there was dual use. So he made available one of his fields at Froghall Farm by the side of the railway embankment. This was a level field with a subsoil of clay so that a relatively true wicket could be rolled out. Howard was a great believer in the application of Nottingham marl and it was not long before a first class pitch was obtained. The outfield was cut by mower regularly and a wooden pavilion was erected, large enough for separate team changing rooms and an area for teas. Toilets (bucket variety) were at the side. This was plush for the age.

It is not known who financed this but Howard Gazeley was key and he allowed Freddie Brightman, one of his workmen, Friday afternoons off to cut the outfield and prepare the wicket. So Flitwick Ramblers Cricket Club was born in the 1920s. A classy cricket ground seems in keeping with what was 'the Jazz Age.'

The excellent facilities attracted many players from other clubs so, with local district players, Flitwick Ramblers was a force to be reckoned with. Dick Dillingham concludes: 'When war came in 1939 it must have nearly broken Howard Gazeley's heart to have to plough up the whole of the cricket ground to aid the war effort.'

Records from this time to after the wars are somewhat vague, and it was only the minutes of a meeting held on October 24th 1949 in the Iron Room in Station Road where we can see a definitive date of the birth of the club. The minutes record that the stated object of the meeting was to discuss proposals for forming a village cricket club. At a meeting held one week later, a proposal 'That Flitwick Cricket Club be formed' was carried unanimously.

THE HOWARD GAZELEY TAPE

In 1987 Nigel Washington recorded a conversation he had with Howard Gazeley, who was born in Westoning and was a prominent figure in local cricket and a significant figure in the history of Flitwick Cricket Club. Nigel's aim was to capture something of the man and something of what cricket was like in the early part of the 20th century and particularly between the wars. Here follow some reported excerpts in Howard's own words:

'I was 15 when I broke into Westoning's first XI cricket team in 1911. Westoning were the team in those days, beating the likes of Ampthill and Toddington. It wasn't real cricket because of the pitches. You could not play cricket on them as we understand cricket. In those days Flitwick was an umpty bumpty old place.'

'Wickets in those days were shocking. Understand this, the fair would come to Flitwick with its engines on wet days and cut deep ruts across the field. What could you do? It was no good for cricket. They worked hard to get wickets and then on a Friday night you would get up there to find boys playing on it. One local game between Pulloxhill and Westoning resulted in Pulloxhill scoring 4 runs, (2 leg byes, 1 bye and one run). The following week Westoning played Harlington and they were out for 7.'

'The ground at Flitwick would be cut twice a year with a horse and mowers. There was a tin hut and behind it Daniel Webb's rhubarb patch. You turned up in your togs, general cricket gear. Underarm was the way to bowl. Overarm bowling was deemed unfair. I was playing in one district match and the ball zipped up and hit me under the chin and I was pouring with blood and as I came off my shirt was covered with blood and Bella Willey fainted!!'

'The atmosphere at a game was unbelievable. Nobody around at a Fair understood the game. They wanted you to win but they hadn't a clue about the game as they wandered about. Some had their own bat and ball but there was a club bag.'

'Flitwick played in a league in the early twenties and their team is the one in the clubhouse with me and the Gaylors and Rol Carr, the blacksmith. It's taken backing onto Steppingley Road. After that there was no cricket played there until after the war. That's why the Ramblers started in the twenties.'

'Anyway after the war we were playing against Aspley Guise up the Westoning "rec" and they were a posh side. One got hit in the eye and he got a black eye. One got hit on the elbow. One of our guys had to have two stitches.'

'Just after that I fixed up with Luton Town to organise a match on Wardown Park and we so enjoyed it there. The hidden skills of our players were able to be shown. Because of that people said "wouldn't it be nice to play on good pitches?" Well we said, let's have a meeting. What are we going to do about a ground? Well I said the only place I know that's flat is my ground down the other side of the railway but it's a bit out of the way. Can we get a wicket? Bert Alsopp is the captain of Beds and professional at Luton and got the wickets prepared. He said you could get a lovely wicket here.'

'So we all put a bit of money in, built a pavilion and I fenced the whole place in so we didn't get any cattle in. We had a really good pitch down there. The pitch was cut using a horse pulling the mower and the horse had leather shoes on it so it didn't damage the surface. And we raised some money with a fête and we had 1100 people there!'

'We had a jolly good side. We got so we were playing Wescliffe, Margate, Putney in London, and all the local teams and Oxford City. We played on the college ground the day after the Australians had played the Universities.'

'We recruited players from all around and for this game at Oxford we got this professional from London so we wouldn't be disgraced. We took a coach over and on arriving we had our bags carried for us by the students!! We weren't used to this as players often arrived on bicycles. Blow me down if the professional didn't get bowled out first ball! But I got 68 and Harry Horsler got 40 and we made a good fist of it and made over 200. But we were beated, but not by much. It was a good day out.'

'We played midweek and Saturdays. Farmers got up early so they could play.'

'That's how Flitwick Ramblers finished at the Second World War.'

Some years after the war there came a knock at my door in Froghall. It was Len Davie and your father (Ted Washington) and a couple more. They'd come to see about reviving a cricket ground and club in Flitwick. Well I said we could but what about the pitch? I don't know who's going to play on it like it used to play unless you want to end up in hospital. They cajoled me and others and we worked really hard to re-establish the pitch at the old Recreation Ground at the corner of Dunstable and Steppingley Roads. (Centre of the table now would be on the Tesco Store petrol forecourt.)

'It's a great game cricket. It's a character former isn't it? You look forward to playing and you practise all week and you go out on a Saturday and you get a rotten stinky umpire and he gives you out LBW when you are about 3 yards forward. You are knocked down to nothing aren't you? And you have to wait another week.'

'And another thing you have to remember. Cricket was terribly important to play because people didn't have anything else for entertainment.'

Back Row, left to right:
Eric Washington, Ron Jeeves, Howard Gazeley (Jnr), Peter 'Doc' Duncan,
Cliff Gazeley, Dave Minns, George Smith (Umpire)
Front Row, left to right:
Bill Wynn, Eric Bonner, Len Davie, Ted Washington, A N Other

In 1951, exhaustive enquires were made into the history of the club nickname, 'The Otters' and club badge of an otter on a crown. There are rumours of the possibility of otters once frequenting the river Flit which runs along the west side of the ground. Despite an upturn in the otter population however, no sightings have been made in recent years.

Nothing definitive was discovered, however, the club crest of an otter atop a crown does appear to have some links with the Brooks family and the Brooks family coat of arms. The arms are 'Or a cross per pale gules and sable'; the crest, 'On a Mural Crown, an Otter Proper'; the motto 'Ut amnis vita labitur' (Life glides on like a brook). The associated Brooks coats of arms are recorded in Sir Bernard Burkes General Armory – Ulster King of Arms in 1884 and registered at Flitwick Manor.

Minutes of a meeting held in March 1951 indicate that this was to be the accepted link.

In the same month, a note is made reminding the club to contact the Headmaster of the local school, Flitwick County Primary, to ask for the return of one ball and to ask for good behaviour of the children regarding the table.

In December 1953, the club joined the Club Cricket Conference, an organisation to which it still belongs today. The CCC helps to find fixtures for clubs who do not have anything organised for the weekend, often at very short notice. In recent years this has provided the club with a mixture of good, bad and indifferent opposition, but it is not known what sort of games were produced in the 1950s.

In March 1954, negotiations took place with the football club for the use of the football hut and a recommendation was made to the AGM to reduce the minimum age of joining the club to 15 instead of 16 with the aim to encourage school leavers to join. 50 years later and with the club now running under 8, under 10, under 12, under 14 and under 16 sections, one of the challenges faced is how to retain those 15 and 16 year olds before they go off to Higher Education and discover the company of the fairer sex and beer!

In October 1954 the club sporadically ran a third XI for the first time. Further negotiations with the football club and the council had to be made for approval and Bert Williamson was asked to captain the team. It was at this time and into 1955 where the ambitions of the club started to rise, with the club investigating the purchase of a new sightscreen and the payment of 10 shillings per week to have the table cut.

October 1956 saw a three year extension of the lease of the ground from the council and in 1957, the first suggestion was put forward to make A and B teams with each section appointing and running its own team. The minutes record that this was not carried at the AGM. 1957 saw an increase of annual subscriptions to £2 for adults, £1 for under 18 and the first forming of a ground committee of Tom Aylen, John Butler, Mick Hardy, Robin Cook, Royston Arnold and Howard Gazeley Jnr.

In January 1958, Mr Stansfield (Club Chairman 1954–1957) passed away and the first memorial trophy was donated in his memory. The Henry Stansfield trophies are still awarded annually today. Members also passed a proposal to switch from A and B teams to 1st and 2nd which would take effect from the 1960 season.

It was in June 1959 that a sub-committee was elected to look into obtaining a new ground. Even then the club was always looking to improve.

KEY MOMENTS IN THE 1960S

Back Row, left to right:
Michael Cherry(Umpire), Colin Banks, John Butler, Tony Jones,
Barbara Waller, Graham Waller, Gerald Olney, Robin Cook, Bill Hall (Umpire)
Front Row. Left to right:
Phillip Jeal, Brian Waller, Brian Miller, Mick Hardy, Mick Sinfield

January 1960 saw the club purchasing a set of gang mowers
for £100 and at the same time, a hand mower was obtained in
exchange for the club's two old mowers. In May of the same
year, there was opinion within the club that the standard of
cricket was going down, and the Rec was becoming unsuitable
for a good standard of cricket. A special meeting was to be
arranged to include 'The club cease to use the Rec for home
fixtures and play all games away for the 1961 season until such
time as a suitable home ground becomes available'.

At the club AGM on the 14th October 1960, it was
noted that there was a decline in membership. A momentous
proposal was made at this AGM that the club should play
cricket on Sundays as well as Saturdays, with away fixtures
only. This was voted on at the meeting and carried with a 19 to
1 vote. As a result of this decision, the Reverend Ball resigned

after considering his position as President. It was not until March 1961 that Mr F S Franklin was unanimously voted as the club's new President, a role he held for only seven months before being replaced by Howard Gazeley senior in October 1961.

The search for a new playing field and sports pavilion continued, with Mick Hardy, Andy Summerfield and Len Davie representing the club at council meetings regarding the possibility of an alternative cricket table on the playing field next to the Rec, but in 1962, the club discovered that a new village hall was not to be included in plans for a new playing field. However, a 20 year lease was requested for an area which was to include two football pitches, three tennis courts and a cricket table, with the football club agreeing to re-arrange the pitches in a way acceptable to the cricket club.

Remember, this was all before the arrival of the supermarket and other buildings, with no modern changing facilities back then and unlike today, when most players seem to have at least four pairs of gloves, two pairs of pads, six boxes, three helmets, two sets of whites, two pairs of boots and five bats, assorted grooming and skin care products and a small pharmacopoeia all carried around in what seem to be large travel suitcases. Equipment was often squeezed into a large canvas bag and carried from fixture to fixture. This equipment would be shared by all players and the canvas bag would very soon be divest of all contents, which would lie strewn on the floor in an ever-expanding area. Getting all the contents back into the bag at the end of the game was always a challenge, and there will be many older cricketers who will have suffered the ignominy of having to pack the bag at the end of a game having been the player who had recorded the lowest score in the game.

In May 1962 work began on the playing fields and it was in June 1962 that Len Davie proposed the club should create new sub-committees responsible for different activities within the club and abandon the system of a control committee. A format that remains in place to the current day, although now a single management committee oversees each of the sub-committees.

In October 1962 at the club AGM, Dr Peter Duncan was elected as the new club president. Dr Duncan was to have a major influence on the progress and development of the club and he is remembered within the current pavilion, with the umpires' changing room being named in his memory.

In 1963, the playing field project was getting further and further behind and the club agreed to look elsewhere for a piece of land. A new ground sub-committee reported that land behind Steppingley Hospital was not big enough. The mushroom field opposite the hospital had possibilities but draining and services would be very expensive (some things don't change all that much!).

In November 1963 a new draft constitution reducing the proposed Sports Club (cricket, football, tennis) to an Association was discussed before going forward to the Parish Council for approval. In January 1964 the Sports Association would come into being and was approved by the Parish Council in February, with the proposal to be put forward to the New Village Hall development committee. The new ground sub-committee continued their search for appropriate land but in June 1965, it was reported at a meeting of the Sports Association that the cricket club could not fulfil its plans to lay a square if the New Village Hall was built on the playing field. Things relating to the new ground went very quiet for a number of years and it was not until 1967 before plans were seen by the New Village Hall Committee at which time the cricket clubs asked for modification to the showers.

March 1967 saw the club sell its gang mowers to Pulloxhill Cricket Club for £110 with a new set being purchased by the club for £190 together with a spiker rake for £10. Compared to the prices of equipment today, these sums may seem quite small, but don't forget, £100 forty plus years ago was a substantial amount of money.

Dr Peter Duncan, President 1963–1991

KEY MOMENT OF THE 1970S.

Arguably the most important period in the history of the club.

Back Row, left to right:
Peter Hopley, Andy Summerfield (Snr), Ken Walters, Martin Ridgley, Bob Lee, Geoff Clayton, Nigel Washington.
Front Row, left to right:
Phil Shaddick, Mick Sinfield, Mick Hardy, Rex Andrews

At the end of the sixties, Flitwick Cricket Club was a thriving little enterprise. Fundraising was an integral part of running the club but it also helped bind the players together. The camaraderie of club members during these events is a good example of how the club has thrived and grown over the years with the input of many, rather than just a few. Membership was increasing and 63 different players represented the club in the 1970 season. Just two years earlier the club had switched to the New Village Hall for changing facilities. This was a step up but still required players to crunch their studded boots across the car park and into the playing field.

We now had a county player in Dave Coleman and there was a sense that our cricketing abilities as a club were being recognised. It was at about this time that the club was making strenuous efforts to create a pavilion in the western corner of the Recreation ground. This would have involved seeking grant aid. So the future was looking good albeit within the constraints of being a village club playing on a public ground with all its attendant drawbacks.

1970 proved to be a fateful year. Mr John Lyall, one time owner of the manor and owner of the Recreation ground and all the acreage to the west, was looking to sell it for a housing development and the cricket ground was included in the sale, the land designated for shops. The news was a shock and caused a deep sense of injustice. The ground was central to the Flitwick village and it offered a gathering place and a focus. The Cricket Club, the Parish Council and 30 individuals registered objections but what resistance were they against the might of big business, property developers and bad planning?

The club first team joined the Millman Cup competition in 1970 and in 1973 the competition was extended to second teams with the club winning their league of 5 games with an unbeaten record and maximum points. This was to be the very first trophy that was won by any team in the club.

To build a pavilion was now impossible so, as an interim measure the club bought a wooden shed to act as a pavilion. This ex-shop facility which, despite its meagre appearance, was placed in the village hall car park to the south west of the ground was regarded as quite an addition to the kudos of Flitwick Cricket Club.

The years blur the inconveniences and embarrassment we experienced because of our limited playing circumstances. Who today would consider entertaining Huntingdon Town Cricket Club and asking them to share changing facilities with the footballers? At tea time, as the footballers completed their shower and wandered naked, who would enjoy asking the opposition to sit in the changing rooms for their sandwiches as the main committee rooms and Village Hall were in use with a jumble sale?

This happened more than once or twice and it was embarrassing. Yes, Flitwick were known as a good cricketing side (in 1971 over 77 matches were played and only 16 were lost). And the club had a reasonable wicket, but no doubt many were saying, 'but have you experienced their facilities?'

In 1972 it was confirmed at a public meeting in the Village Hall that building permission had indeed been granted on the Recreation Ground. This did not provoke a sponsored pub crawl around 8 local pubs but it might have done. How times have changed, but indeed the club did have 17 brave and thirsty souls who got themselves sponsored to drink a unit of alcohol at each of 8 pubs. And more than one lap was completed by some to raise the princely sum of £140 for the club's coffers. For some it was a busman's holiday.

A northerly view across the Rec with electricity sub-station

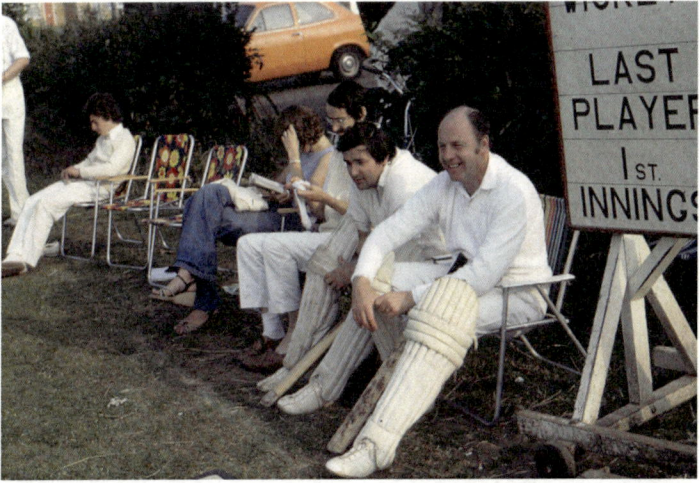

Rod Young, Dave Moules and Tony Jones alongside the club's mobile scoreboard

Dave Moules driving the roller

An easterly view across the Rec toward The Swan public house and railway bridge

A southerly view of the Rec with Andy Summerfield Snr batting

STRENGTH IN ADVERSITY

Although there was a threat to the very existence of the club in the mid 70s, it would be easy to argue that it was never so strong as in those days of uncertainty. There was thriving membership with 144 attending the annual dinner and dance and this was coupled with a spirit of enterprise and forward thinking amongst the players and supporters.

Committee meetings were normally held at Andy Summerfield's home in Maulden and they were always run efficiently and effectively with high expectations of committee members and excellent record keeping. From such professionalism was born the strength to move forward as a cricket club.

When many others might have given up hope, seeing the prospect of the club existing 5 years later as highly unlikely, this band of 'brothers' never surrendered the torch handed to them by previous generations. No, these meetings were places to give account, to proffer suggestions, and to share ideas of how Flitwick Cricket Club might live on. Thank God for these men, for without their collective spirit what is now would not be.

WHERE CAN WE PLAY CRICKET NOW?

A westerly view taken from the bridge over the railway line, on the corner by The Swan, looking back to where the cricket ground used to be

In 1974 negotiations continued with the idea of purchasing five acres of land adjacent to the railway line off Windmill Road. The cost was to be £12,000 which was more than £10,000 more than the club had in the bank but, with grants, it might be possible. Underlying the exciting prospect of having our own ground was the reality that the five acres in question were far from ideal. The shape of the ground would have been a little odd and weren't we paying over the odds anyway?

1975 produced a very hot summer with 88 of the 101 fixtures played. Colts fixtures were beginning to be arranged and although there was the threat to the very land we played our cricket on, we were not surrendering hope but were moving forward.

No grant aid was forthcoming for the Windmill Road site for a new ground, but out of the blue an alternative was found next door to Flitvale Nurseries. Confidence was high that purchase could be made in the next couple of years and the will was there to do it, even though scaremongers and prophets of doom said we would never play cricket in that field as it flooded each winter and the soil was wrong!

The committee met on the ground one hot evening in September 1975 and knee high in grass in places they ruminated. Every picture tells a story and the photo taken by Nigel Washington tells a story of men with the weight of destiny upon their shoulders. Shall we? What if? Can we afford it? We'd need a pavilion. Bear in mind that the club received absolutely no recompense for having to leave their previous site.

In the Spring of 1977 work started on the drainage of the ground, a topic which has never really gone away to this day!

Thoughts and worries proliferated. Seen here in Nigel's photo are club members Mick Hardy, Graham Wynn, James (Andy) Summerfield, Tony Jones, Geoff Clayton, Phil Shaddick, John Butler's pipe and elbow and Ken Walters considering just those thoughts. Surprisingly, the identity of the person wearing the small white hat and sunglasses is to this day something of a mystery!

To raise the monies required to purchase the land and start developments, a new ground fund was established, John Butler introduced a new 250 Club, and 150 people attended a Fur and Feather Whist Drive. The push was on. A new ground was in our sights. In true Flitwick style, the costings for this venture were carefully planned and thought through, with the details of what was needed recorded on a piece of card, using different coloured pens. The following picture is that original piece of card. No spreadsheets in those days!

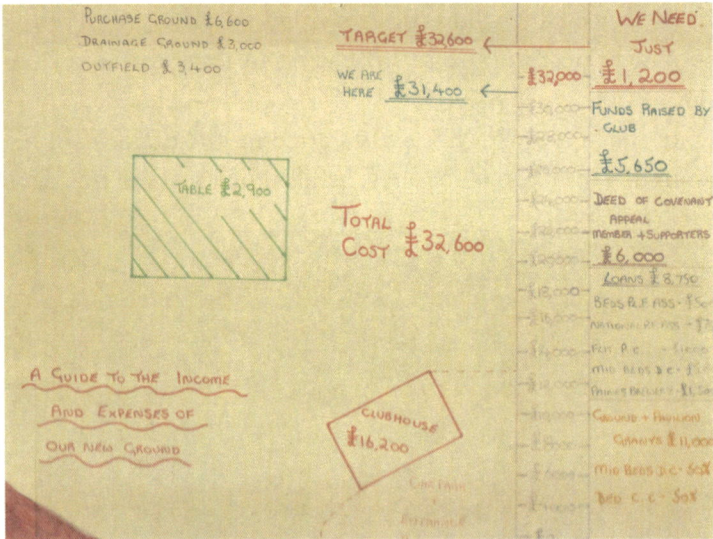

Whilst it is a bit difficult to make out, what can be seen is that once again the closeness of the club members and the effort put into finding different pots of money from many sources, show that out of a target of £32,600, £31,400 had been raised. These efforts continue to the modern day, with club members foraging the financial opportunities available through sport funding, as evidenced with the grant of £24,000 received from Sport England in 2012. In fact, between the years of 2001 and 2013, over £85,000 has been spent on ground and clubhouse improvements.

1976 produced yet another giddy summer of heat and activity. Remember the brown outfield at Lord's that year? On the cricket front the first XI played 2 of the most amazing games in its history, firstly recovering from the jaws of defeat at 30-6 to beat Henlow who had posted 191. Graham Wynn posted an heroic undefeated 125. If that wasn't enough to stir the blood and confirm that league cricket was capable of generating brighter cricket, Papworth, for 3 seasons the kings of Millman Cup cricket, smashed 273 explosive runs on the Recreation ground and declared after 40 overs. In an astounding fight back Flitwick won off the fourth ball of the last over with 275-7. These were unforgettable games which signalled a new brand of cricket.

Obviously a new pavilion would be required and the club invited 5 different companies to tender. After much deliberation and discussion, the contract was awarded to Trevor Battams at a cost to the club £10,100.

The team that played the last game of cricket as Flitwick Cricket Club at The Rec.
Back row L to R: Roger Butler, Dave Moules, Bob Smith, Simon Andrews, Chris Howard-Cramer, Mick Shiner, Charlie Eadesforth
Front row L to R: John Farrant, Keith Taylor, Nigel Washington, Neil Kelliher

BRINGING IN THE MONEY

As the club has developed over the years, funds have had to be raised from numerous sources. Several club stalwarts have spent many hours completing a variety of application forms for a share of pots of money that are available hidden away in the dark recesses of various organisations. These days, the income generated by the hiring of the clubhouse is a major source of revenue, as well as generous sponsorship from local businesses.

The 1950s saw the occasional jumble sale but its main fundraising came from monthly whist drives in the old 'Victory' village hall alongside the cricket ground. Various organisations took their turn at running the drives which at the time were very popular. The main event of the year was the Christmas 'Fur and Feather' drive with club members being allocated village shops and businesses to beg whatever possible as prizes. The most profit made on one of these was the princely sum of over £44 which at the time seemed a fortune.

The 60's saw a change, in that the whist drives waned and in their place bingo became the main source of extra income. Four squads formed a rota giving their time every four weeks to run the evening's event. Each squad comprised of 4 to 5, each having their role to fill. Caller, money handler, runner between tables, tea maker and washer-upper.

A 400 club was formed in conjunction with the football club with the idea of each club finding 200 members at 10p a week each, with a weekly draw. Although the cricket club found itself collecting from far more than their allocated 200, the profits were shared. Eventually the cricket club went it alone and over the years the format was changed with fewer members and a greater weekly sum collected. This became the bread and butter income for the club.

The Victory Hall – scene of many fundraising functions

Luther Bradbury, Phil Shaddick, Peter Hopley, Chris Howard-Cramer, Ivan Dix and Kevin Hayhurst at the Good Friday 20 mile sponsored walk refreshment point

'Hubbie' Short – astute fundraiser

Profits from these events appeared adequate to keep the club solvent but time was running out with regard to the tenancy on the ground known as the 'Rec'.

There had been several attempts to buy or rent a new site to convert into a cricket pitch, none of which came to anything. Whilst the 'Rec' was available to us the urgency and drive to find that new site was not there. This was all about to change.

The minutes of a management meeting held in May 1976 record the decision to purchase the new ground which was timely as the council gave the club notice to quit in September 1978 but gave an extension of one year after discussions. The importance of this stage of the club's progress was indicated by the 52 meetings held in 1977. Not so many today!

It was very quickly realised that having had notice to quit the 'Rec', not only was there a need to find a new place to play the game we all loved, there was a need to raise a lot of money and very quickly.

A professional fundraiser was contacted who came from London to a meeting. This was to see if we could work together and swell the coffers to not only buy a plot of land but to erect a clubhouse on the site. Compared to previous activities, this was to be a mammoth task. The fundraiser, John Turner, was a very likeable chap with a positive attitude and although relatively new to the job his 'get up and go' rubbed off on the club members. Our financial arrangement with him was 10% of all takings were his.

A fundraising committee was formed with John leading the way and various events were planned. The first thing he created was a 'Deed of Covenant' with the majority of the club pledging monthly sums of money. This released a sum from the bank which enabled us to buy the present ground.

John worked with the club for two years and in that time taught us not only new ways to raise money but sums we had never contemplated before. An example of this was an ambitious 'Go-Kart Derby', held on local farmland in June 1977. The Karts were rented for the day with each Kart sponsored in each race along with the races themselves having a major sponsor. A risky venture as it was unknown what public response was to be. Having well advertised the day we could only hope, not only regarding public response but weather too. We need not have worried, the day was a great success.

In the 1960s one ambitious event organised was a 50 mile walk comprising of a figure of eight route with Flitwick being the cross over point. The majority completed 25 to 35 miles with one young lad covering the full 50 miles.

Good Friday was often an occasion for a sponsored walk and in the 1980s and 1990s John Butler and Chris Matthews planned routes across a multitude of fields and through various woods of Bedfordshire. The 20 mile walks were always well supported, with upwards of 80 club members taking part with their families

Check points at various stages on the route involved the planning and delivery of hot and cold drinks and added entertainment was provided by a series of cryptic clues requiring solving en route. Back at the clubhouse at the end of the walk, answers and further refreshments were provided for the weary walkers. The final amount of money raised would be announced, with this figure often being around the £1,000 mark and a significant contributor towards the costs of running the club.

The feeling of everyone pulling together took the club through the stage of being an everyday village club to a well-organised and professional sporting unit.

As sponsored walks became stale, despite the route being varied, a fresh form of traditional Good Friday sponsorship took place. These involved 12 club members playing indoor games for 25 hours. A timetable was created telling each member what he was to be playing for any given hour. The games comprised carpet bowls, snooker, dominoes, darts, skittles and the occasional hour rest. The main aim was of course to get sponsored, with each having more than one sponsor card assisted by other club members, wives and friends widening the catchment. This format was eventually changed to exercise cycle machines, again with the 25 hour endurance. It turned out to be a punishing 25 hours, never to be repeated. A financial success but many injuries and aching limbs.

Two other sponsored ventures were created, horse race nights and duck racing. Six wooden horses were made and 'jockeys' were to wind an attached cord drawing the beasts to them. Horses and races were sponsored; also various forms of betting took place which again brought in another source of income. These evenings passed with a great deal of merriment with the bar being well used.

The club bought 100 small plastic ducks and 10 somewhat larger. The banks of the river Flit were cleared of overhanging bushes and branches and any rubbish for a quarter of a mile upstream. The smaller ducks were numbered and bought by members and friends. The larger ducks, again numbered, were bought but at a much higher price, creating an 'executive' race within the main event. This usually was held on a club barbeque evening in the summer. A net was placed across the Flit at the finish line level with the clubs boundary. Ducks, large and small were cast adrift upstream and allowed to flow at their own pace eventually arriving in sight of Flitwick Cricket Club's ground. Great excitement ensued, especially after a drink or two, with the winners of large and small ducks receiving a prize.

One form of raising money has seen the test of time. This is the great-great-grandson of the aforementioned 400 club. It is now based on the bonus-ball of the weekly national lottery. It has moved on somewhat in that in the 70s it was 10p a week, collected by hand. Today it is £1 a week, set up on a bank standing order, just another example of how times have changed.

Mock auctions were a useful source of disposing of unwanted items, although caution had to be exercised by those attending. It was at one of these auctions where an example was seen of how not to bid for an item. The auctioneer was offering an old tour T shirt with an opening bid of £2.00. An incredulous voice was heard from behind the bar, '£2.00??' to which the immediate response 'sold' was called and the barman became the somewhat bemused owner of a probably unwanted and quite expensive T shirt.

It wasn't all funds from the club, however, and significant effort was made filling out forms to obtain loads from various breweries including Benskins, Ind Coope, Paines, Greene King and others.

The fundraising couldn't stop and it didn't. A record £1,200 was raised for the Good Friday walk and a further £1,000 was raised at Andy Summerfield's third Summer Hoe Down. The business side of the club was well organised and the emerging new facilities could thereby flourish.

Things are somewhat different today, with fewer fundraising events being organised. Barbeques and quizzes still prove popular and groups of supporters make regular monetary contributions by braving the elements on the patio area during and after games over a glass or two of refreshment discussing where the players went wrong, who should be batting where, why player A should be bowling instead of player B and how the standard of fielding has let them down again and why don't they practise more ... and on ... and on, just like this sentence.

BUYING THE NEW GROUND

The decision to purchase the new ground was taken in September 1975 with the official purchase taking place during the ensuing winter at a cost of £6,000. The Club was then faced with the task of raising £23,000 to complete the Clubhouse and ground development. Momentum was huge, enthusiasm rife as the immense challenges were undertaken often with the talents of those within the club. The land was actually purchased in May 1976, with the Clubhouse shell planned to be established in the winter of 1977/8, with 4 months then allocated to get the internal work completed before the new season. Graham Wynn was a driving force in keeping the club members motivated, making sure that jobs were done on time.

Playing on the ground was not anticipated, but the reasoning was that if the Clubhouse was in place it could generate monies for the completion of the whole project and so it proved. It also generated the most amazing team spirit with members offering their skills, working together for their club. So many were so selfless and was the Club ever happier?

So many club members were able to offer their talents and practical craftsmanship. We had builders and electricians, shop workers in hardware, draughtsmen, technicians and accountants, farm workers and those knowledgeable on soil and drainage. All needs were met it seemed.

Not everything went to plan but planning went into everything. There were rumours at this time that the A5120 that runs alongside the ground would be straightened at some stage in the future which would mean taking a corner of the ground. Negotiations with Mr Frank Brittain, the previous owner of the land took place to purchase a further acre to maintain the amount of land required. The road straightening never happened, but the extra acre proved invaluable to the club.

ALL OUT—NOT FLITWICK !

All smiles in front of the new club house. Left to right Flitwick Cricket Club members Graham Wynn, Barnard Simms (fixture secretary), Nigel Washington First XI captain) and Dave Moules.

FLITWICK CRICKET CLUB could have been hit for six after it was learned the ground they had played on for many years was to be swallowed up in new town development.

But the club, founded in 1902, was determined to carry on and members have been working hard fund raising to re-establish the game on a six-acre ground just over the border with West oning.

A magnificent pavilion has been built for only £16,500. Much of the work was done by members themselves.

It overlooks what will eventually be one of the best cricket grounds in the county, but it will be many months

yet before a ball is bowled.

"There's another £5,000 worth of work to be done before its playable in 1980," said first eleven captain Nigel Washington.

Meanwhile cricket is still being played on the old ground next to Flitwick Village Hall.

Notice to quit has been given by the site owners. Although cricket may continue there for the present season, next year's fixtures remain uncertain.

Last year the club raised £800 at a go-kart derby, at Greenfield.

It proved great fun for people of all ages. A bigger and better Go-Kart Grand Prix will be held at Greenfield on Sunday, July 2, in aid of the cricket club's ground development appeal, when it is hoped about £1,000 will be raised.

An excerpt from an article in the Ampthill News of the time

Hard work was the order of the day and work parties were born.

The table and outfield were scheduled to be completed for the 1979 season. However, because of finances and delays and the need for the table to mature, the reality was that the ground would possibly not be ready until 1980 season. The Club had been given 29th September as the expiry date on its lease on the Recreation ground so the Club was in something of a dilemma. Subsequently an extension was granted but at one time it looked as if we might be that rare type of cricket club, owning a ground and a clubhouse but having nowhere to play!

In 1977, 52 official meetings were held concerning the Club's new ground. Fundraising ventures continued. 2,000 people attended a Go Kart derby at Phil Tookey's Moat Farm in Greenfield, sponsored walks and draw tickets, Hoe Downs at Andy's farm, the list of ventures goes on. It was impossible to turn up to a cricket game without someone like John Butler saying 'Have you got your ticket?' Or 'How's your sponsorship coming along?' It was all good sociable fun and very profitable. It needed to be.

This stage of the history of Flitwick Cricket Club was an era when the true togetherness of the club was never better exemplified. The amount of work that was put in on a voluntary basis, together with the support of friends and families is very difficult to put into words. The well-known phrase 'a picture tells a thousand words' could not be more apt here.

Using Bob Dunning's considerable knowledge and skills, along with a good deal of his machinery and equipment, what follows is a pictorial section which shows just what was achieved. To this day, Bob continues to provide work on the ground, maintenance of equipment and he is yet another example of the unsung heroes of the club.

Summer 1975 on the evening the decision was made to purchase the Vale

Andy Summerfield spraying the wild vegetation

Trevor Battams, Mick Hardy and Phil Shaddick 'checking the drains'

Ground levelling and raking

Graham Wynn and David Butterworth de-stoning the new ground

A gradual slope engineered to the Nursery End

'You'll never play cricket there' – the cry of the locals

John Butler and Mick Hardy survey the table

The meadow land intially looked like a field of cricketing dreams

Bob Dunning civil engineering comes in to play

Bernard Simms at work

Building the foundations of the clubhouse

Starting to take shape

Ready for the roof

Unloading pipes donated from a nursery in Eaton Bray

Mick Hardy in the trenches. NB. Hardcore in place in the table.

CLUBHOUSE OPENS

On 26th May 1978 the new ground Clubhouse was officially opened by our then president Doctor Peter Duncan, who also pulled the first pint of bitter from the pumps supplied by the Paines brewery in St Neots. For his part he had taken on the role of 'Capability Brown', appearing at committee meetings with plans of where a whole range of trees and shrubs might be planted to enhance the beauty of the ground, especially for when he might visit in later years from above, atop a cloud. This event was also attended by Sid Morris who was the Secretary of the Bedfordshire Playing Fields Association who was a valued supporter of our efforts to launch this facility.

The Clubhouse had been completed with all its fittings within 6 months for the cost of £15,500, a remarkable achievement by 'a band of brothers' with a common aim. This included support from local businesses such as Wallspan Bedrooms who provided many items free of charge to the club.

Everyone enjoyed the clubhouse. Like children with a new toy they kept on trying it. On a Friday night it would be packed with members and friends playing darts, skittles or snooker and talk at the bar continued until the volunteer barmen called time.

Still the New Ground Committee was meeting sometimes twice a week as the completion of the ground itself was orchestrated. 1979 promised to be the last season on the old Recreation ground. The cricket continued. Malcolm Wynn joined the club and he and Nigel Washington each scored 1,000 runs that season. Roger Butler won the Colts Duncan Batting Cup. This was the first year of the Mid Beds District Youth League which was founded by Mick Hardy and his colleague from Ampthill CC, Pete Smith with Colts teams drawn from Flitwick, Ampthill, Silsoe, Aspley Guise, Eversholt and Eggington. These were the early seeds of what has blossomed since.

SETBACK THEN FORWARD TO THE FUTURE

In 1979 an abnormally dry autumn followed by an abnormally wet spring meant the grass seed was prevented from germinating. This was a setback, as was the inability of Goff and Son from Oakley, to complete the formation of the square on schedule and to the Club's satisfaction. So the Club decided to complete the task from its own workforce. In the centre it was something of a mess. The ugly smelling clay which had cloyed the square had to be removed, hard-core had to be tossed into the depths of the ground in preparation and the appropriate soils laid as a base. At times the square had resembled a swimming pool and this only fuelled the critics and cynics with ammunition.

The outfield though was soon looking good with Golf Landscapes managing to level the land, seed it and fertilise it so that, but for the square in the centre, some semblance of a playing arena was in place. The ground was landscaped with a slope to the southern end by the right of way to aid viewing and when the grass grew the images of giant diggers and trailers faded and we began anticipating the prospect of cricket on our own ground.

Already the clubhouse was being used for teas in matches played at the old Recreation ground and opposition teams marvelled at the ambition and vision that were bringing a cricket ground to life from what was a field of grazing horses. Even before cricket was played on the new ground Graham Wynn was cajoling his committee to go for an extension to the lounge. The scorebox from the 'Rec' was changed to include a scoreboard, and the dressing rooms were furnished as the club moved to play on its brand new ground in 1981. It was all systems go! Flitwick Cricket Club, 'The Otters' moves into its first proper home, 'The Vale.' There was much rejoicing and probably not just on Earth but also from stalwarts passed on watching from cricket fields in the sky.

THE 1980S AND ONWARDS

Now that the club had the ground, pavilion and scorebox in place, development took the form of additions such as covers, sightscreens and general improvements to the facilities. As before though, these things didn't simply just happen and a lot of work was completed by the unsung heroes of the club.

So many small but important jobs were completed by club members and it was during these times that, yet again, the camaraderie and team spirit of the club shone through as it had on many occasions before and indeed since.

The big news of January 1984 was the resignation of the club from the Millman Cup competition and 2nd X1 league. This followed a resolution at the Millman AGM to make all clubs play one another in a 3 tier league with promotion and relegation. Flitwick Cricket Club's proposal to allow each club to choose its own fixtures was defeated and, following the decision by Flitwick Cricket Club not to offer a certain team fixtures for 1984, the only course of action was to withdraw from the league. All fixtures against league sides would be played under Millman rules but would not count in the league.

In January 1981 work was still ongoing on the clubhouse extension with volunteers needed for Sunday morning toil. Funds for the work were still being sought from a variety of sources. 'We can only furnish the club according to the money that is available.' Match fees rose to £1 and players were urged to share transport costs with drivers to away fixtures.

Ground development continued with new sightscreens, additional netting and a new 14 inch mower planned. Mick Shiner was appointed part-time groundsman assisted by Horace Billington. Club playing members would still be needed to assist, however.

COMMUNICATIONS IN THE CLUB

In February 1959 Flitwick Cricket Club produced *The Flitwick Cricket Club Magazine* a 'new magazine' to give news of the club and its members and to give something extra to those who watched or read newspaper reports of the club's exploits. It listed forthcoming club activities and, at the price of 6d, was not intended to make great profits. It was intended to publish again in March and then from May through to September with one winter edition in December. Readers were invited to submit ideas for a title for the magazine.

In the first edition there were reports of ground improvements (6 tons of muck to be spread on the Rec), the introduction of the Duck Tie (awarded for 3 successive ducks), jokes, news of John Butler joining the Merchant Navy, club finances, the hire of a taxi to take players to away matches, the search for more umpires, the donation of the Stansfield trophies, puzzles and a social diary. The social events covered were the St Valentine's Old Time Dance at Redborne School and, at the same venue, the second annual dance with mainly modern dances plus a few old-time ones. One dance raised £40 and was attended by 200 people, the doors having to be closed at 10pm. A piano recital was given in the interval plus a half-hour of skiffle from Luton's *The Vampires*. Whist drives (13 over the winter) were the main fundraising events, with the Fur and Feather one at Christmas being well attended and generously donated to by local traders and the wider community.

The second edition in March contained much of the same but also a *Spotlight* section profiling a leading player and a few snippets of news about players and fixtures. By edition 3 in May 1959 (editor M J Hardy) the magazine had the title *Rambler*.

The first edition in February had sold 95 copies but had failed to cover printing costs. A new cover had been designed but was not used until June and the editor's column contained the following advice: 'If you can't have the best of everything, make the best of everything you have'. The Treasurer (apt initials LSD) made pleas for more funds as running costs for the club were high. Selected quotations from literary works were used to illustrate club events and characters, e.g. 'John Butler scoring a boundary "clapped their little hands with glee with one continuous sound"': 'Longfellow.'

With its new cover June *Rambler* had brief match reports as well as the aforementioned features.

It was not until 1969 that news came to be disseminated again when an Flitwick Cricket Club newsletter was produced advertising indoor net practice at Redborne School on 2 evenings per week. Ground issues were covered and the efficacy of Dave Cheeseman's mothballs as a mole deterrent discussed. Subscriptions were set at 10 shillings (50p) with a match fee of 2 shillings (10p) Teas would cost 3 shillings (15p) per person. A replacement for Charlie Brown as 1st team scorer was being sought as well as a 2nd team scorer.

From April/May 1986 newsletters were produced on a quarterly basis to promote fundraising activities, report on social events at the clubhouse and cover ground and youth section matters. In February 1987 there was news of a forthcoming football match between under and over 25s on Luton Town's 'carpet' and also of the formation of the Otters Golf Society.

Fundraising was again to the fore with forthcoming events including bingo, a mock-auction, a car boot sale and a sponsored indoor games session. April/May 1987 bore congratulations to Mick Hardy on being awarded the Home Counties League Special Award which was presented on April 10th. The report of the football match (a 3-3 draw) and news of the winter indoor nets were also included. Newsletters continued in 1987/8 in a similar vein and then in January 1989 the first edition of *The Otter* hit the market! Where previous newsletters had been stapled together A4 sheets, *The Otter* was an A5 booklet, as *Rambler* had been. A new feature was *Spotlight on the Past* which looked back to events of 1970. Forthcoming events in 1989 were a curry supper, a celebrity dinner and a craft fayre. The growing colts section took up increasing amounts of column space, showing the club's commitment to its junior membership. Football news, golf, cartoons and puzzles made up most of the rest of the content of issues. In the autumn of 1990 there were two significant resignations. Martin Shotbolt was forced by ill-health to give up his role as chairman of the colts section and Nigel Washington ceased being editor of *The Otter*.

February 1991 saw another change of format as *The Otter* became once again A4 sheets stapled together. Still published quarterly, it contained much the same material as previously, with the contributors still trying to raise money, enthusiasm and morale. *The Otter* continued in this format into the 21st century and its features were extended to include the *Player Profile*, a list of achievements, tastes and heroes of a player in each issue. This harks back to the days of *Rambler* and its *Spotlight* section of 1959.

The internet age hasn't put an end to the newsletter but electronic communication is now the preferred medium.

AT THE VALE

The Vale has been used to stage Minor Counties cricket for the Bedfordshire County Club and has hosted the Northamptonshire County Club on three occasions for benefit matches for Peter Willey in 1981, George Sharp in 1982 and Geoff Cook in 1985. Off the field activities mean that the facilities are used by many people over the course of a year and the club is a venue used for parties, wedding receptions and other social events.

As with so many of the developments of the club, the commitment of club members was such that within 5 years of purchasing the land, the first game played at The Vale was a match played between two teams made up of players within the club; a 'John Butler XI' and a 'Geoff Clayton XI'. The first ball was bowled by Mick Hardy, the first ever run was scored by Simon Hull and the first wicket was taken by John Farrent.

The official inaugural game against Dunstable was played on Sunday 19th April 1981. A return fixture against the same opposition to celebrate 30 years of cricket was played on the 18th April 2011 and the changes that have taken place between those two fixtures mean that the home of 'The Otters' is now considered to be one of the best in the county, not just on the playing front but also in the general surroundings, with the club having received several 'in bloom' awards.

The original pavilion consisted of a single bar area with toilets and a kitchen area and two changing rooms. In 1980 An extension to the pavilion was begun. Completed in 1981, the clubhouse has now become a popular venue for parties and celebrations. The bar area has undergone several re-fits, including moving the bar forwards slightly to enable easier movements for the staff working behind it. There was a bar in the lower area which has now been closed off to provide better facilities for cleaning and glassware. On the wall facing the open floor area, there is a cabinet displaying the numerous trophies and awards that the club has won over the years.

The addition of a decked seating area and an extensive patio in 2008 has helped to enhance the facility further. On many a summer day, often progressing long into the evening, groups of families and friends can be seen discussing the situation of the game whilst sampling a refreshing glass or two of their favourite beverage.

Inside the clubhouse, there is now a separate changing facility for match day officials. The room was named 'The Duncan Room' in memory of Dr P G Duncan. Dr Duncan was an active member of the cricket club from the early 1950s to the mid 1990s. He held the position of President of the club and his love of all things horticultural was expressed by his planting and nurturing of a series of trees and shrubs around the boundary and to this day serve as a reminder of a true Otter.

This room was built from the space that was created by the development of an equipment store which once contained all manner of cricket equipment, including many pairs of mis-matching gloves, split pads with rusting buckles, broken bats and stumps, with the occasional useful item being rustled up in case of emergencies. How much of that equipment made its way there from the canvas bag at the old ground is unclear. If you take a look at the outside wall near the corner of the building in the car park on the Nursery side, you will see a slight change of brick colour which shows where the original store doors were.

In 1984 construction of a brick built scorebox started. This was another significant improvement to the facilities at The Vale, and funding for it was helped with a deed of covenant scheme, where 20 club members agreed to pay a sum of money over the course of 8 years.

The scorebox was completed in 1985 with the official opening being conducted on the 9th June in that year, when The Otters staged a benefit match for Geoff Cook of Northamptonshire County Cricket Club.

Seen here are Nigel Washington, Malcolm Wynn, Mrs Muriel Wynn, Graham Wynn and Geoff Cook in front of the scorebox, the fascia of which was sponsored by the Wynn family

In 1990 Nigel Washington became the first player to take 100 1st team wickets in a season. In the same year, Dave Butterworth took 96 second team wickets and 9 in the first team.

Non-turf nets were added to the facilities at the ground in 1992, the introduction of rolling covers and large clear sightscreens in 2003 meant that the standards continued to improve, and in 2011, the facilities marks from both the Hertfordshire and Bedfordshire leagues showed Flitwick to be top of the pile of all clubs in those leagues. This is a true testament from visitors to The Vale of the quality and attractiveness of the ground and its surroundings and a tribute to all the people who have worked so hard and selflessly to provide such facilities.

Over the course of the years, the club has invested in a large amount of equipment. Some of this equipment has not simply been purchased, but put together by the members themselves. A particular example of this was an ingenious set of sightscreens at the River End of the ground. A set of rails along which the screens could be pushed on rollers, all held together with scaffolding. Although now having been removed after 30 years of service, these screens were an early example of the resourcefulness of club members.

A set of regularly used nets and the addition of a roped boundary and covers add to the overall impression of a finely appointed ground. The ground is maintained by club members, and one individual who has worked tirelessly to maintain the high standards of the facilities at The Vale is Mick Hardy. Mick has been associated with the club since the early days and arguably has spent more time at The Vale than anyone else. Despite having recently handed over the groundsman mantle, he still continues to be seen doing his bit to ensure that the ground continues to be a wonderful place to play and watch cricket.

Occasionally after particularly heavy rainfall, the river has been known to burst its banks. Despite this, the ground is well drained, and very few games are lost because of an unplayable outfield. With a garden centre at the opposite end of the ground, the River end and the Nursery end are aptly named.

Around the boundary edge, a number of seats have been donated by club members either as memorials or simply as gifts, ensuring regular stopping places for those who like to take a stroll around the boundary edge during the course of a game. There is an unwritten rule that such perambulations must always be anti-clockwise after tea.

The Vale becomes part of the River Flit – showing the ingenious sightscreen mechanism

PERSONAL MEMORIES

Every club member will have memories of the club and perhaps one day there will be a second tome with contributions from all club members. However, it is hoped that the reader will forgive this little bit of self-indulgence from the co-authors, along with contributions from others who have seen the club in a different light.

Richard Wigfield

I moved to Bedfordshire from Middlesex in 1982. An old school friend of mine, Duncan McAllister and his wife Annie had moved to the area, and we used to visit them at the weekends with the pretence of helping them decorate. The reality of things, however, seemed to include more beer and pizza than paint and wallpaper. It was during the course of these visits that I and my then wife to be, Jackie, realised that we could afford a property in the area. After we were married in 1983, we moved to our first home together in Flitwick and have lived there ever since.

Cricket has always been my summer activity of choice, having played at The John Lyon School in Harrow, and for Hatch End, my local club where I grew up, so it was no real surprise to Jackie (or Annie I suspect) when Duncan and I saw an advertisement for players to join Flitwick Cricket Club in a local shop window and announced that we were going to drop in to see what it was like. Almost as soon as we had put our heads around the door of the clubhouse, we realised that this would indeed be a great place for us to play cricket. It must be recorded here, however, that in our first game for Flitwick, Duncan was considered more of a bowler, and I was considered more of a batsman. Those that know my prowess with the bat will not be overly surprised to know that it did not take the selection committee too long to discover my true flexibility as a batsman, being able to fill the number 10 or number 11 spot with equal aptitude.

As with many clubs, there are other clubs in the local area, and there has long been a healthy local rivalry with our friends at Ampthill Cricket Club. Matches at all levels are always played very competitively, very occasionally become a little heated but the contest very rarely crosses the boundary rope. Players from both teams have often shared a late-night curry and beers away from the cricket arena and indeed the two clubs combined to provide teams for a tour of the West Indies in 1996.

The camaraderie between the clubs was arguably demonstrated most spectacularly in the late 1990s when Ampthill were about to develop and enhance their facilities with a major facelift of their pavilion. Although usually on these occasions, the result is important and gives bragging rights to one or the other team until the next contest, the result of this particular game is secondary to the events that unfolded.

Many club cricketers will remember with some fondness the tradition of buying a jug of beer for the opponents and on this day it became evident that the need to commemorate the old pavilion and welcome in the new meant that the jug would be filled regularly. Very regularly. The jug took the form of a watering can and was filled first by one team, then by the other, being passed with ceremony on each occasion.

As time passed, a number of games took place, including an eating competition between a member of each team. This meant that the floor was starting to receive cracker crumbs, the occasional peanut, pork scratchings and other such culinary delights as a result of the competition, but by that time, it is fair to say that no one was particularly over concerned. It should be recorded here that despite a valiant effort by the Flitwick representative Mark Dallman, the contest was effectively ended with Ampthill's representative and secret weapon, Danny Phillips finishing off a pickled egg in one mouthful.

By now, the jug was being passed to individual team members with reasons for it to be filled becoming more and more unreasonable, but unavoidable for fear of further punishment. The passing of the jug ceremony was becoming more vociferous and animated, with it being slammed down onto the nearest available surface along with a loud challenge of 'THE JUG IS WITH FLITWICK' or 'THE JUG IS WITH AMPTHILL' before being taken back to the bar for refilling. As time went by, various barrels were emptied and by the end of the night, the jug was being filled with pretty much anything that was left. This seemed at the time to be a perfectly rational thing to do, although the full repercussions would not be felt by most players until the following day and for some, the next two days.

Although we do not condone the consumption of such quantities of alcohol, it is fair to say that this night cemented still further the connections between our two clubs. I spoke to my friend Ian Smith, (a true stalwart of Ampthill Cricket Club and indeed Bedfordshire cricket) sometime later after the game. He reported that when he went back to consider clearing up the aftermath of the events of the evening, despite the impression of utter devastation in the pavilion, it had in fact gone a long way to help clear the stock and negate the necessity of the employment of a subcontractor for a small amount of demolition work that would no longer be required.

Dave Moules

I arrived in Ampthill to teach for 3 weeks at Redborne School in July 1968 prior to starting the job full-time at the beginning of September. I was roped in to play in the annual Staff v School cricket match in the last week of the summer term and, having scored some runs and shown some capability, was approached by Graham Lane to join Flitwick Cricket Club. Graham was a member of the Redborne teaching staff and Flitwick Cricket Club 2nd XI captain. He was always on the look-out for players and, over his years at the school, must have recruited at least a dozen staff to play for the club. Some, like me, stuck with it for many years, others played odd games when Graham was struggling to find a full side. I played for a while in that 2nd team on Saturdays and Sundays, later making it into the 1st XI as a lower order batsman, very occasional bowler and demon fielder.

A typical weekend would have one match at home and the other away. Home games would usually involve some contribution to wicket and ground preparation. Andy Summerfield, head groundsman, would arrive on Friday evening to mow and scarify the chosen strip and, over the course of Saturday and Sunday mornings players from the teams to use the 2 strips would complete the marking of white lines, boundary line, rolling and any other tasks. Prior to the match, white tarpaulins had to be fixed to the metal frames of the sightscreens, the 'telegraph' board readied and scorers' tables and chairs set out. During the game we would often have to take a turn umpiring as opponents sometimes arrived umpireless.

At the end of the game what had been got out had to be put away. I cannot ever recall doing any kind of warm-up or warm-down exercises beyond throwing a ball around in a rather haphazard way as we emerged from the changing room in the village hall. Those with cars parked them in the hall car-park, ensuring that the space they used was on the side furthest from the hedge boundary to the cricket field. Many cars not parked as carefully suffered hits from balls launched for six, I being responsible for a few, as well as hitting a passing car on Dunstable Road.

Tea was taken in the hall and my connection with the school eventually gained me the task of procuring girls to prepare the teas. Some did both days, others one, but many Redborne students gave sterling service at the Rec and, later, at The Vale when we used the new clubhouse for teas prior to starting to play on the ground itself. In addition to sourcing the caterers I was also responsible for sourcing the raw materials for tea from Pete Robinson's shop in Windmill Road. When the sun shone and the match went ahead all went smoothly but, a last-minute call-off meant letting all involved in the tea routine know of the cancellation. Before the days of email and texts this could be a long and time-consuming task. To finance the teas and their preparers I would also collect the players' match fees on the day, pay the tea-girls and pass any balance to the treasurer or team captain.

Away matches were somewhat more relaxing, although match fees still had to be collected and tea money paid over to the opposing captain. We would often be travelling quite long distances and Peterborough, Corby, Warboys, Ely and North London were regular haunts. My knowledge of the Fens was of help when we were trying to locate grounds and pubs and especially fish and chip shops on the way home. Yaxley, near Peterborough, was a regular stop for refreshment. In pre-breathalyser days a fair amount of alcohol was consumed even by the drivers.

One car always had to carry the club kitbag with its assortment of pads, gloves, bats, boxes etc. Few players had all their own needs although, gradually, fewer and fewer made use of the club kit. A great tradition of the club was that the lowest score of the day had to pack the bag at the end of the game, ensuring all pairs of pads and gloves etc. were accounted for. We have all had that task and have also said to ourselves 'Well, at least I'm not packing the bag' on scoring a run to overtake the lowest scorer or seeing a team-mate dismissed for a lower score than ours. During the days between matches the kitbag usually was stored by the captain at home or by the person in whose car it had been transported.

A later innovation was the 10p fine for a dropped catch. When a catch went begging there was no sympathy or admonishment but a chorus of '10p, 10p, 10p' from one's fellow fielders. A diving attempt to get fingertips unsuccessfully to a half-chance met the same fate as a chickening out of going for a skier because 'I lost it in the sun'.

When we played at home we went to one of the local pubs after the game. In my days we used The Wheatsheaf, The Crown and The Blackbirds, different captains preferring each. The landlords/ladies were usually happy to accommodate up to 30 good drinkers any Saturday or Sunday. Dominoes became very popular and regular challenges were issued and accepted, especially involving our umpire, Perce Burrows and his mate and arch-seller of 'swindles' (scratchcards to raise funds for the club) Hubby Short.

Fundraising tended to be quite low-key until the new ground was mooted. Due to be turfed off the Rec, we had to purchase a site, but to develop it to our spec would require some serious fundraising. Players and supporters rallied round to take part in a myriad of sponsored events such as walks and snooker marathons. 'Mock' auctions (with me as auctioneer) were organised. Our professional fundraiser chivvied us on and the money duly came in.

When we weren't fundraising we started to develop the ground. A swimming-pool (the table-to-be) was a source of great local interest as it filled with old roof tiles, brick rubble etc. to help it drain freely. The clubhouse took shape and eventually we could move in for teas and after-match socialising.

We were also now responsible for running a bar and most players took their turn on bar duty. This was normally done in pairs and we opened at first on several nights per week, with Friday, Saturday and Sunday always very busy. Often the team playing away would turn up back at the clubhouse to report on the game and top up with another pint or so. Having a bar also meant ensuring that stocks were adequate and I, John Butler and Ivor Newbury would take turns to check stock each Monday and get the order to Mick Hardy for him to pass on to the suppliers. We got our beer initially from Paine's of St Neots, where you could buy three pints and still have change from a pound, a brewery now long gone.

The local populace found out a lot more about the club in those days as The Ampthill News was still going strong and gave good coverage to local sports clubs. Reports would be written on sheets provided by the paper, with scorecards duly filled in and comments appended. Another task which often came my way as I lived in Ampthill, was to drop the reports on Sunday evening into the letterbox of the Ampthill News office in Church Street.

As the ground neared completion and the first fixtures played we rightly felt very pleased with all our efforts, but we were soon to find that other developments were needed. The sightscreens were coming to the end of their lives. The metal frames had been welded many times and, on the larger ground, were not really adequate. Some new ones were proposed for the River End and, once again, my school connections came in handy. The plan was to have screens sliding on rollers on a track. John Butler did a design and 'acquired' a large ingot of steel for Joe Lyons, head of Technical Studies at Redborne, to turn into the items required on his lathes etc. These were duly handed over and fitted.

Over the years the clubhouse has provided pastimes to help drinkers to enjoy their evenings. Dominoes (there was a knockout tournament) became very competitive as did snooker. Space Invaders occupied some (especially Geoff Clayton) and the fruit machine did good business. During matches many non-batters and dismissed ones would indulge in a 'pondle'. This word was introduced by me to the club. I believe it to be a bit of old Fenland dialect but it may well be something I picked up from a relation or local yokel in my young, impressionable days. A 'pondle' is a relaxing stroll and usually took a group around the boundary edge, often putting the world to rights as we 'pondled'.

There was a great sense of camaraderie in the club and we always had 'characters' who brought their own sense of fun and love of the game. Some people with whom I played are now dead and gone but many made a significant contribution to the building and development of the Flitwick Cricket Club which flourishes today.

John Butler

During the 50s, 60s and 70s a typical village scene could be witnessed by standing on Flitwick railway bridge and looking west. At weekend afternoons and the occasional weekday evenings, a cricket match would be in progress on what was affectionately known as the Rec.

A 3.5 acre recreation site given over to village use with an accepted arrangement that Flitwick Cricket Club, for a peppercorn rent, would maintain a central square for wickets and keep the surrounding grass cut.

Alongside the ground stood the village hall erected after the 14-18 war which in the early years was used for club teas, annual dinner/dance, their fundraising whist drives and bingo evenings.

Beyond the hall was Daniel Webb's field, containing rows and rows of lovely rhubarb. The ball regularly found its way amongst the ready to pick sticks, much to the annoyance of the owner.

Shared with the football club was a Nissan hut behind the hall where players changed and during the overlap of football and cricket there could be as many as 44 bodies jockeying for position. The soil floor did not help to keep cricket whites in a pristine condition especially during rainy days. Beyond the hut the club's mower, along with various other equipment, had storage in a ramshackled old lean-to.

Memory says we had no problems with this relatively insecure arrangement but it would be difficult to imagine safety being maintained today.

With the playing area being relatively small, balls were hit out of the ground on regular basis. One of the most peppered spots was over Steppingley Road and into railway property. This was known as Charlie Brown's garden. Charlie lived in the railway house and was usually the 2nd team's umpire. Calling the area 'garden' is giving it too much credit, undergrowth may be a better way to describe it. Therefore finding a lost ball required a considerable search party.

The hedge separating the ground and Steppingley Road was a great spot to watch cricket from and there would appear a regular line of heads. These heads seemed to melt away the moment a collection box appeared on the scene! It was said that the Swan's landlord offered a fiver for anyone who could break a pub window with a direct hit. This feat was never achieved so the challenge was never put to the test.

Soil conditions on the Rec were such that the morning of a game could see a thunderstorm with torrential rain but a match would still be possible by the afternoon. There were no wicket covers in those days and there were many occasions when the wicket was put to the test. Due to the light sandy soil one problem was always ongoing, just as it is on the present ground – moles. The little blighters churned up the outfield which had an undesirable effect on the gang mowers.

Three non-playing members from those days deserve a mention. Charlie Brown was one, the other two are Perce Burrows and Hubby Short. They enjoyed their cricket just as much as any players. Perce umpired for many years mainly for the 1st X1. Hubby will be best remembered for his appetite for fundraising. Three great characters whose names will always be associated with the club.

Flitwick's population in the early 50s was around 2,500 exploding to over 13,000 at the last census and attaining town status in 1978. Dramatic changes to the town meant the cricket club was also forced to change and so the 'Vale' was born. When looking from the railway bridge now the only remaining features from those distant days are The Swan, Dunstable and Steppingley roads, now with a roundabout separating them.

To try and place old features with new will not be accurate but for some idea the old village hall was somewhere near where the entrance is to Tesco car park. The wicket around the exit from Tesco and I like to think I ran up to bowl where number 6 petrol pump is sited!

That poor old rhubarb field has Tesco store dumped on top of it and our rhubarb comes in tins!!

Nigel Washington
MY DREAM OF TEAMS

Knowing this book was being written and contributing to the writing of the history has made me quite nostalgic for those days gone by when as a teenager the smell of linseed oil laced with a waft of horse liniment was enough to keep a young and fanatical cricket enthusiast stirred with anticipation of a game soon to be played and heroics soon to be performed. In my time with Flitwick Cricket Club, first as an eager 13 year old, called in to make up the numbers in the 1st XI and then some 50 years later 'wheeled out' in the President's XI, I have been privileged to play with some wonderful personalities and distinctive cricketers. Consequently I wondered if I might select the best eleven cricketers I saw representing Flitwick. Another idea was to write about my favourite personalities in the club over the years. In the end I have decided to do neither because in my view personality is inextricably woven into ability on the cricket field. So in the end I have decided to randomly trawl my mind for those with whom I have had the privilege of playing cricket and who have left a rich and warming memory for me.

No doubt I shall miss some important folk out and for some my assessment may be totally wrong. The editor may censor the piece. But what I offer is a partial and thankful reflection on some people I have had the immense privilege of sharing time with on and around a cricket field.

GRAHAM WALLER was a blond haired, left arm spinner and skipper when in 1964 he warmly encouraged me into the team when I first played for the club. He even gave me a couple of overs when the game was almost won. From those early moments I was so impressed with Graham's ability to flight and beguile. I also respected his gentlemanly qualities.

His brother BRIAN WALLER had a long career with the club and served it well on and off the field. He played cricket with a smile on his face and his medium fast bowling was always a rich mixture of experiments. An over could be filled with inswing, outswing and slower ball long before the fashion of today's limited overs games. Brian loved his cricket and was never shy of offering advice. 'If you weren't wearing that fancy cap you would have caught that one!' was one gem offered to me, and he was probably right.

MICK HARDY was always an exciting player to watch. Before I began playing I revelled in watching this very fast bowler speed across the ground and deliver skidding accurate deliveries which often brought a haul of wickets. He had a lovely action which repeated efficiently and this saw him play through many decades, gleaning a record haul of over 2,000 victims, a total that will never be beaten. He was a shrewd respected skipper and in time has emerged as 'Mr Flitwick Cricket Club' with fantastic devotion and wisdom invested into the club at all levels. He was a motivator and worker for the new ground. He has always been a trusted colleague on and off the field to so many and he is respected far and wide in cricket circles. My understanding with him is encapsulated in the times we batted together and pinched singles, just with a look and a nod. True understanding I felt.

ANDY (JAMES) SUMMERFIELD taught me more about cricket than any other person. He was a stylish and pugnacious batsman who had a compact style and excellent pull and hook shots. He was something of a run machine through many seasons, his Bedford School coaching proving effective. If he opened he regularly saw the score to 50 believing a good final score is built on sure foundations. He prized his wicket and competed like few others. As a wicketkeeper he was excellent, often standing up to the wicket to fast bowlers and supremely alert for stumpings. He was for many years the best wicketkeeper in Bedfordshire and in a less elitist age would have played many times for Bedfordshire. Andy was a tiger on the field, cajoling the fielders and eager to outsmart the opposition batsmen. Off the field he was a gentleman and a clubman of the top order. Our current ground was purchased and developed only because Andy's guiding hand was involved. We owe him a great debt.

JOHN BUTLER was also a significant motivating force for the new ground. Both as fundraiser and practical worker he advanced the ambitious project along with others. A key figure in building the camaraderie, I was grateful to him for introducing me to midweek cricket when he created teams at Wrest Park. Like me John was not a natural cricketer but he was someone who made the most of his abilities and applied them to devastating effect at times. As a seam bowler he brought the ball down from a good height and contained batsmen with unusual accuracy and subtle variations. Bowling maiden overs was commonplace and, finding little scope, batsmen often succumbed. John also delighted in fielding at short leg wearing no shin pads or helmet, often breathing on the opposition batsman in anticipation of a catch. John's last game of cricket was alongside his son and grandson. He cherishes that. Marvellous.

DAVE MOULES began in the first XI as a middle order batsman who would vigorously club spinner and fast bowler alike to midwicket, given the chance. Today it would be called the slog sweep. In Dave's playing days it was something of a 'moo' but no one in our team complained because it was mightily effective. Dave also played a good range of weighty orthodox shots with his trusty Clough and Ward. Dave then became a prolific off-spin bowler with a beautiful combination of length ball being followed by one apparently tossed up for a free hit. So many a batsman fell for that one. Dave was an excellent all-rounder and club man. When returning from games to the East of England Dave's car always seemed to veer to the fish and chip shop at Yaxley and once during a game he improbably dug out a burrowing mole from the outfield. Moules molests mole!!!

MALCOLM WYNN and I didn't always see the game the same way but there was no doubting his cricketing gifts. A stylish batsman and bowler he also fielded well and had a brilliant throw which surprised many a batsmen attempting a run on the throw. Malcolm had a wonderfully high action when he bowled, he could seam the ball either way and if provoked a little he could make the best of batsmen jump. As a well coached batsman Malcolm had a wonderful array of stylish shots. He was always reluctant to play an ugly shot;

in fact I can't remember him ever playing one and he scored many a fine run for the club. Now he is helping others to do the same as groundsman.

BRIAN INGRAM joined Flitwick Cricket Club when we came on to the new ground. As an opening batsman he was pugnacious and stylish and the better wickets drew out his natural cricketing talent. A genial and wise cricketer he excelled as skipper securing the confidence of his players and demonstrating a brave attacking style which was prepared to give the opposition a chance of winning, if it gave his team a better chance of winning in the process. As a wicketkeeper he was excellent and his quick responses and good glove work brought many a stumping and catch. For me he once caught Alan Lamb which I shall always appreciate and a magnificent hook shot off county bowler Brian Marvin lingers in the memory. As Club Chairman he has presided over a challenging more professional era whilst upholding the traditions of the club.

GRAHAM WYNN was a stylish cricketer and first class fielder. Fleet of foot he used his footwork to good effect when batting and his cover drives were a touch of class. In the field he was eager and frequently he would cajole others to be on their toes. One of the club's most memorable matches centred around Graham's prowess. At the crease with Flitwick 30-6, chasing 200 at Henlow, Graham launched an assault which was still spoken of decades later. And he finished on 125 not out as the game was improbably won. At 30-6 two Henlow villagers left the game saying, 'It's not worth watching. Flitwick are pathetic.' Oh to have seen their faces on reading the sports page of the local paper later in the week. Graham was an exciting player on the field and he was an exciting player off the field. He was such a massive driving force for the development of the new ground. He had vision, he would always push his colleagues on to achieve more and as chairman he was respected and valued.

MICK SHINER was nicknamed 'Shonker', a corruption of his name and batting style for he was in some ways 25 years before his time. Mick hit the ball from the off and scored many runs. He was most in trouble when he tried to defend! A little hesitant when the ball was hit towards him he nevertheless didn't mind thumping it very hard at others. Mick dealt in boundaries and rarely troubled himself with singles. Once I tried to gee him up for a single but Mick resisted and a wag from the pavilion shouted out, 'you can't rush the council!!'

LES WARD seemed to walk straight out of a public schoolboy cricket annual with his dashing strokes, joy for life and love of cricket. He always looked to impose himself when opening the batting and his quicker than average scoring benefitted the side. I enjoyed opening the innings with Les as we seemed to have an understanding even if that meant we ended up on occasions discussing it from the same crease as the fielding side whipped the ball in to the other end!! Les played with a smile on his face and he was an asset to the club.

MICK SINFIELD was a mildly truculent cricketer who bowled slow medium seamers which were almost unplayable on a damp wicket. Not a natural athlete Mick was nevertheless a good slip fielder. Mick often bowled with his shirt open to the waist and with medallion swinging merrily before him. Unusually he also wore his watch on the field as well. Once, a batsman who was obviously mesmerised by Mick's approach to the crease, asked him to do his shirt up. Mick placed his hands into the teapot pose and was obviously not best pleased. Mick also had spells with Ampthill.

MARK HALL broke into the first XI as a teenager and during his career his free flowing strokes made him a good and consistent scorer for the second team. He also bowled in the early days and his ability to swing the ball by bowling off the wrong foot hauled him some useful wickets. A good clubman Mark was in some ways our first overseas player, coming as he did from Australia.

Mark Hall – first Australian to join the club

Andy Summerfield Jnr - prolific batsman 31,000+ runs and still counting!

POP WHITE was a hero of mine when I watched cricket in the 1960s. Although a fast bowler when he played at school, for Flitwick he was a big hitter. Muscular and relaxed in the face of opposition bowling he would strike the ball great distances. Rather sleepy in the field he nevertheless had great reactions and seemed to catch the ball when it was flying past his ear. I enjoyed playing with him and once opened the innings with him chasing only 90 or so runs which Baldock had mustered. When the game was won by 10 wickets I was not out 9 as I recall!!

DAVE COLEMAN was a class cricketer who performed brilliantly in all departments. The most stylish of batsmen, he scored quickly, an occasional bowler he was very quick with a final leaping pen knife action and as a fielder he was sharp. Quantity of runs forced him into the county side. I shall always appreciate the encouragement he gave me as a spin bowler.

RICHARD WIGFIELD was an excellent opening bowler who, when in his pomp, could trouble the best of batsmen and frequently did. Possessing an ability to swing the ball late, Richard bowled a very full length and enticed batsmen to start fishing. A modest man he worked hard for any team he played in and retained an optimism whilst others doubted. I must come out and say that Richard is the only man I have hugged on a cricket field, this when the first XI snatched victory from the jaws of defeat to enable the winning of the Bedfordshire League.

TONY JONES was the most positive captain and player I played with at Flitwick. Every game could be won in his opinion, no cause was lost. Flitwick were the best team in the county. In truth he had a very good team around him so he was right to have confidence. His own batting was hit and miss. He had a terrific eye for the ball and he used this to wipe fast bowling off a length to the far corners of the leg side boundary. I recall batting at number 9 in a game at Harpenden and I carried an instruction from the skipper of the day to Tony. 'Skipper says play for a draw.' 'OK' Tony replied before upping the tempo and slogging us to victory.

The ANDREWS Brothers. Rex was an obdurate opening batsmen in the golden team of the sixties. Rex would lay a platform for the innings and with determined defence he would look to blunt the opposition fast bowling so that the following batsmen could reap dividends. Terry was a stylish opening batsman with a range of shots. An all-round sportsman he was also a more than competent left arm spinner and slip fielder.

ANDREW SUMMERFIELD junior has become a legend in his own playing days. I first remember his neat fluent batting style when he was in his teens. Over the years he has become a real run machine accumulating scores with apparent ease. He has served the club in a manner of which his dad would have been proud. As colleague, captain, Cricket Committee Chairman and as a link between generations, Andrew embodies all that is good about Flitwick Cricket Club.

DAVID BUTTERWORTH brought a northern edge to the 1st X1 when he joined the club in the 70s. A careful and correct left hand batsman he was more than useful down the order but it was his swing bowling initially and then his wicket to wicket stock bowling which drew success and a hatful of victims. Dave is a cricketing optimist.

GEOFFREY CLAYTON was a cricketing enthusiast who enjoyed plenty of success, mostly in the second XI, though he did keep for several seasons in the 1st X1 and also captained the side. Geoff should chiefly be remembered and honoured for the sterling work he put in as treasurer and enabler when we transferred grounds. He worked very hard as financial adviser.

BERNARD SIMMS has Flitwick Cricket Club running through his veins and his contribution to the club has been immense. Bernard never sought the limelight but he was always amongst the first to volunteer for duties however difficult or menial. As fixture secretary, tour organiser and 3rd team leader he was supremely good. Meticulous and hugely enthusiastic he carried others with him on his enterprises. He became the first club member to be a qualified umpire and he took this responsibility very seriously. A staunch family man he would be the first to acknowledge the part they played in his loyal fully involved role in the club. Bernard was not a top cricketer but few were keener and I delight still in the 50 he scored against Coopers in Berkhampstead one sunny afternoon in the 1980s. A top Otter.

CHRIS MATTHEWS is the current stalwart of the club with his countless contributions to its smooth running. He is a superb treasurer and as well as distinguished service on the Clubhouse Committee and the Bar Committee, Chris is now also helping with the ground preparation as Ground Chairman. Chris has been a very reliable club cricketer. A stoical batsman he never struck terror into the opposition but he was capable of accumulating lots of runs though I still can't believe it I once saw him take a hat-trick at Axminster!

These are just a few of the players who come to mind. There are many others I could recall and revere: Trevor Alcock with his swashbuckling innings against Hemel, Charlie Eadsforth, a gutsy and talented all-rounder, Andy Thoseby, with fast late in-swingers to please any captain, Simon Hull, full of technical belief and pugnacious runs, Nick Olney's style and excellent fielding, Martin Hull's brave keeping, Andrew Woodcock with dobbing spinners and mighty batting assaults, Chris Howard-Cramer with 100% commitment to bowling and fielding and many many other wonderful Otters. But for now they will have to wait for the next book to be published or another's recollections.

Phil Gurney

'FROM OUTSIDE TO IN'

As a real young lad, I recall several 'away' matches to Flitwick as my father played when Sandy travelled to the 'Rec' with Mr Fage in tow as the most competitive man I had seen! After one such match when I would have been 9 or 10, I recall Nigel proudly showing us, as the opposition, around a concrete shell and barely grassed field of what was to become The Vale.

My earliest memories of games at the great ground were from the scorebox, with Pipsy as my oppo scorer, as I watched some sporting pitches keep scores very low as matches were shared between Sandy and Flitwick.

My first appearance in whites at The Vale is strikingly familiar and recalled as if it was yesterday – if only I could be 15 again! I remember so clearly a Sandy player named Martin Pettitt being stopped for speeding through Caldecote on route to The Vale! The day got no better as Mr Hardy and a 'recovering from injury' Mr Wigfield helped themselves to five wickets apiece as Sandy 2s were dismissed for a paltry 45, with just a single run contribution from a young opening batsman. The Otters knocked off the runs in no time, with a 'dropped' Summerfield not even getting to the crease! A very vivid memory was however after that game, as Flitwick declined what at the time was a traditional 'beer match' to opt to have a team net practice instead – only in later years was I to realise that professional approach was the way to play the game! Before the night was out, Maradona had punched England out of the World Cup to complete a thoroughly miserable day!

My own move to Bedford Town in 1993 allowed me to progress my cricket, and again matches against Flitwick and at The Vale are strong in the memory, but in the Bedfordshire Premier League. Ridiculous catches by Twist seemed a regular occurrence, the cashing of Bernie Vouchers if things got a little tight, Nigel headbutting the final ball of the match to secure a tie, and the Hospital Cup trilogy of matches all feature. Those Hospital Cup matches, when it was a proper competition, were real hard fought affairs – with some very narrow matches featuring, usually thanks to Mr Wigfield's bowling. For one of those semi-final matches, I was lucky enough to be skippering the Town team and walked out to toss up with Andrew Summerfield and was simply amazed at how fantastic The Vale looked on a summer's evening. I asked him who was looking after the ground – Mick Hardy of course was the answer!

The visual impact of The Vale, the professionalism of how the club was run, and the competitiveness of the playing side, were already firmly etched in my mind when what ended up being my final match for Bedford Town took place in June 2000. With Flitwick being reduced to 38-6, our skipper decided not to take the game seriously and The Otters cashed in to win the game easily. I wanted to be part of a club that did things the right way, on the pitch, off the pitch, always progressing, always demanding success. After a committee meeting or three to decide if they would let me in, the rest as they say, is history!

Steve Davies
'COMING UP THROUGH THE RANKS'

I had started playing the sport at school aged 9 and it was a school friend Jamie Wade who suggested I come and play at Flitwick Cricket Club with him. That was in 1990 and when I first turned up to a net practice I am sure I did not imagine that I would still be doing so 23 years later! When I look around at the Vale now I am always struck by how lucky we are to have the facility that we have, but as a 10-16 year old you tend to take these sorts of things for granted! No, my earliest memories are not of the picturesque ground or the hard work people put into the club, but of my first colts team manager Jason Twist bowling at me in the nets. With every leave outside off stump the ball would come down a little faster (it is tempting to suggest bigger no-balls were bowled too but I can't prove that!) and I was given a proper working over by the end of the net session! It was a good place to learn and get tested and I looked forward to that little challenge each week at practice.

I played with some great players as I came up through the ranks and some friendly advice from an experienced hand was never far away. An early memory, from what was possibly my first 1st team appearance in a midweek game at Potton, though involved some less than friendly advice! I was around 14 or 15 and was keeping wicket for the first time to our West Indian overseas quick bowler Charlie Morris. The first ball of the match got a think snick from the batsman and I remember clearly having it under total control ... until it thudded straight into my chest and dropped to the floor. Charlie glared and muttered loudly 'this is big boys cricket' and walked back to his mark at an incredibly slow speed shaking his head continuously. I played many times with Charlie in subsequent years of course and I am pretty sure he forgave me!

Flitwick was a great place to play as a colt in the 90s. There were opportunities to play plenty of cricket and progress into adult teams. The balance between encouragement and support and either being worked over in the nets or knowing you were playing 'big boys cricket' was always just right and an important part of my development as a cricketer I am sure.

OTTERS ON TOUR

The cricket tour was always a week that seemed to take a long time to arrive, but passed in moments. There is an old saying that 'what goes on tour stays on tour', and some stories must remain that way. However, the tour was always an occasion for players and partners to get away from it all for a few brief days, and to experience the hospitality of other clubs and their surrounding area.

The chief organiser of the club's tours was Bernard Simms. Bernard is a man of character, and took no nonsense on the field of play as one of the first fully qualified umpires at Flitwick Cricket Club. Sometimes outspoken, but always valued, Bernard was able to pull together the necessary arrangements for a group of upwards of twenty people on various cricket tours. This included accommodation, fixtures and all the fine details that others would have missed.

Getting to the games in the first place was often quite an achievement in its own right. The idea of everyone sticking together in a convoy of cars was often replaced with a small gumball rally style of travel, with no-one except those well prepared travellers having any idea of where we actually needed to be.

Tour matches were always an opportunity to find a way of getting people to contribute to an after match fund, even if they didn't want to. One of the main ways of extracting money was a series of fines that were levied during the course of a game, and it was on tour that the largest amounts were raised.

The first official club tour took us to Devon, with visits to the Cotswolds, Kent and Wales also featuring. There are doubtless other clubs who have visited the Lynton & Lynmouth Cricket Club at the Valley of Rocks ground. A spectacular venue, where players can be easily distracted from the game by the magnificent surroundings. At our visit there in the mid 80s, a small group of players decided to cross the road to watch the top order batsmen rack up the runs by climbing one of the hills opposite the ground. After a brief trial run, we worked out that we needed to start applauding when the bowler was about 5 yards away from delivering the ball, so that the sound would reach the players just after the batsman had played his shot.

Tours took place from 1983 with the first trip being to Devon. A visit to The Cotswolds in 1984 was followed by a trip to Kent in 1985. The popular journey to Devon was taken in 1986 and 1987 before venturing north to Yorkshire in 1988 and 1989. Back to Kent in 1990 and 1991 before the first venture out of England took The Otters to Wales. Tours to the Principality took place in 1992, 1993 and 1994, before returning to Devon again in 1995, 1996 and 1997. Visits to Lincolnshire in 1998 and 1999 were the last time the Otters toured.

Bernard Simms 'Ready for action, pal!!'

THE DEVELOPMENT OF YOUTH CRICKET

Youth cricket at Flitwick in recent years has been an outstanding success, with over 130 youngsters on the books of the club, playing in organised age groups from Under 8 to Under 16 sections. Under Howard Moxon's guardianship, the Colts section is one of the best-organised and well-run sections in the county. Results may not always go the way that would be liked, but the spirit of cricket and the emphasis on enjoyment of the game are strong messages that are passed on to future cricketers.

As with so many things at Flitwick, however, it has not always been this way. 1979 saw the first year of the Mid Beds District Youth league which was founded by Mick Hardy and Pete Smith.

The colts sections grew and began to produce young players who would battle their way into the senior teams and men such as Martin Shotbolt were to make sure that the principles of fair play and sportsmanship were nurtured and encouraged. For whatever reason though, membership began to decline, and whilst games were still played, it was becoming clear that something needed to be done. In true Flitwick style, it was decided that the club would fund the provision of qualified coaches, which had an immediate effect on the standard of practice and subsequently of the games.

Cricket was finding new young players, and the 2005 Ashes series proved to be a major factor in the number of young players wanting to try their arm at the game. To be able to benefit from this, the club took the bold step of running two colts teams at each age group in the club.

This obviously put a strain on the coaching and team management resources of the club, but, as always, club members and parents took the bull by the horns and mucked in to help. The standard of coaching got better and better, with the inevitable result of better players producing better results and in 2007 an under 15 team from the club became the first team to represent Bedfordshire and progress to the latter stages of a national knockout competition, beating previous winners along the way before falling in a closely contested quarter-final match to Hadleigh Cricket Club, representing Essex.

I wonder how many reading this can remember asking the club coaches if they could travel down the night before and stay in a hotel before preparing for the big game the next day. Needless to say, that idea was quickly quashed and an early start on a Sunday morning in the Sea Scouts minibus was the order of the day.

Back row left to right: Richard Wigfield (Coach) Ben Barzilay, Andrew Bloxham, Pierce O'Mahoney, Mark Umlauf, Liam Peters, Joe O'Donnell, Howard Moxon (Manager)
Front row left to right: Aaron Kennett, Josh Nicklin, George Thurstance, Dom Moxon, Chris Fenney

It is worthy of note that, at the time of writing, seven of this team are still playing senior cricket at Flitwick. Today, youth cricket continues to provide young players with the opportunity to learn the game. For several years now, the backbone of the club's three senior teams is made up with home-grown players who have come up through the ranks.

One of the first Flitwick Colts teams

THE FUTURE

This history takes us to the 30th anniversary of the opening of The Vale. It was always going to be difficult to decide on a cut off point for inputs and there are some references to things that have taken place outside this scope. Work has of course continued after this time and will continue in the future.

The game itself has changed dramatically over the years and Flitwick Cricket Club has embraced and indeed championed some of these changes as evidenced for example by the fact of being the first club to wear coloured clothing in the Bedfordshire League. As a club, there have been developments both on and off the field of play, and I'm sure that this will continue in future years.

A strong and vibrant youth section will without doubt be the lifeblood of the club and the steady stream of young players moving up through the year groups and into senior cricket will continue to be an integral part of the future picture. Not just from a playing point of view either. There will no doubt be future umpires, scorers, committee members who will come through to take over roles and responsibilities within the club.

Flitwick Cricket Club has been blessed with the input and vision of many dedicated members and parents who have given up their time freely to ensure that the club is able to offer the opportunity for people of all ages and abilities to play cricket. The work of these people includes roles from Chairman of the Colts committee, through team managers and coaches to providing transport to and from games, refreshments, support and advice. As long as this dedication continues, the future of Flitwick Cricket Club remains sound.

As far as the standard of cricket is concerned, well, no-one really knows of course, but the club has made significant progress over the years, and there is really no reason to see why this should not continue. The facilities at the club are second to none, and the dream of the addition of a second ground would go a long way to help spread the load on the current facilities. It would also lead to the further development and raising of the standard of cricket and in turn, the profile of the club within the community.

What is unclear, however, is the shape of the game to come. The longer game seems to hold less attraction, and certainly the costs involved will continue to get higher. No longer featuring extensively in state schools, it is only through the efforts at grass root level of clubs like Flitwick that the game continues to thrive. We feel that the stewardship of the club is in good hands.

ACKNOWLEDGEMENTS

This book owes much to the input of many club members, and the team of co-authors is grateful to those who have made this history.

Organising and facilitating cricket for young people remains a challenge with the large numbers that the club attracts. Providing a safe and enjoyable environment was originally started by Mick Hardy and in recent years by Howard Moxon. Their foresight and continued efforts with the support of coaches and team managers have provided the youngsters, who are the lifeblood of the club, opportunities that they would otherwise not have had.

As with any sport, the game cannot take place without officials and the club has been fortunate to have enjoyed the services of many qualified umpires, scorers and coaches who have all officiated regularly at many levels within the structure of Flitwick Cricket Club and also within the structures of the leagues in which we play.

Mention must be made to the long suffering wives, girlfriends, partners of the players. The ladies of Flitwick Cricket Club play their part in many and varied ways, including participation on committees, input to the maintenance and appearance of the clubhouse amongst others. Mostly, however, it is the support and encouragement that they provide which has helped keep us menfolk on track (most of the time!) for the benefit of the club.

The majority of work done at the club over the years has been purely voluntary and it is important to recognise that there will be many people who are not mentioned in these pages who have also made significant contributions in some way to the development of the club. The work of these unsung heroes and heroines continues today, not just on the field of play, but also with the off-field activities of those committee members, family and friends who give up time to ensure that the future of the club remains strong.

Thank you, all of you.

Richard Wigfield
868 wickets taken bowling right handed
7 taken bowling left handed
2559 Runs
149 Catches

APPENDICES

CLASSIC EVENTS

The Loo Seat

A splendid example of the relationship between Flitwick Cricket Club and our friendly rivals is a wonderful bit of tomfoolery which began in 1994, when a cricket match was arranged to be played between The Otters and our local friends and rivals Ampthill Cricket Club. Although unconfirmed, it is entirely possible that this plan was hatched late in the evening after a game between the two teams and perhaps a glass or two of refreshment, when I'm sure it seemed to be an excellent idea at the time.

The decision was made that the game would be played on Boxing Day/New Year's Eve, regardless of what the weather was. 20 overs per side with each player having to bowl at least one over – perhaps an early concept of T20 cricket? We like to think that the match played on the 31st December 1999 was the last game of cricket played in Bedfordshire and possibly in the country, in the 20th Century. Links with local schools have meant that the games have been played on artificial pitches installed at those schools and the game has never actually been staged at the home ground of either club. I'm sure that respective groundsmen will want to keep it that way.

On one occasion there was some consternation when, upon arrival at the venue, a thick layer of snow covered the whole field. This meant that the first task was actually locating the artificial surface. Experienced eyes were cast across the whiteness, and inspired guesswork led to the discovery of the pitch, at which time shovels and brushes were use to clear the pitch ready for the game to commence.

Passers by may have thought 'only in England' upon seeing such sights as fielders in the outfield holding umbrellas, or

Cricket madness whatever the weather!

Jason Twist receiving the Loo Seat Trophy from Ampthill Cricket Club Chairman Mike Thomas

doing a more than passable imitation of The Michelin Man by wearing several layers of clothing (I'll insert the obvious 'some don't need the layers of clothing' quip here). Batsmen having to avoid snowballs being launched at them at the same time as a cricket ball being bowled to them; 'sledging' taking on a whole new connotation. Perhaps daftest of all though are the spectators who attend to watch the winter madness begging the question who are the most foolhardy ... the players or the spectators?

At the time of this publication, although some records of scorecards are missing, I'm pleased to be able to report that Flitwick have won The Loo Seat on far more occasions than Ampthill!

A few memorable matches

In the history of any cricket club, there are a number of memorable matches and here are just a few.

Cricket is littered with examples of close finishes and dramatic recoveries, but one of the biggest turns in fortune occurred in a fixture between the Flitwick 1st XI and Cutler Hammer 1st XI played at Kempston in a Bedfordshire County League fixture on 3rd August 1997. Having been asked to bat first, Flitwick amassed a total of 167 for 7 from their allotted 45 overs, with contributions of 41 from Jamie Wade and 33 from Paul Arthur. At the time, whilst this was considered to be reasonable total, the quality of the opposition meant that the prospect of a close finish was high.

The Cutler batsmen were soon making significant inroads to the total. With the score at 100 – 1 and the batsmen looking in complete control, some Flitwick supporters (including the club Chairman at the time ... you know who you are!) had decided they had seen enough and left to return to Flitwick.

It was then though that events took a dramatic turn, with wickets falling like autumn leaves in a storm and soon Cutler were reduced to 155 for 4. 13 runs required with 6 wickets in hand and with still plenty of overs left to be bowled. A formality, surely?

Tensions rose as Cutler moved closer and closer to the total, but it was becoming clear that the momentum was definitely with the Flitwick bowlers Bryn West and Richard Wigfield who tore into their opponents in a manner which left some questioning why they did not start like this in the first place. Each wicket was celebrated with increasing gusto starting with a simple stroll to the centre and pats on the back moving through a gentle jog and firm handshakes through to sprints from the boundary, high fives and shouts of joy until the last wicket fell leaving Cutler stranded on 165 all out to scenes of jubilation from the players involved. It was on this occasion that Nigel Washington hugged another player on the field of play for the first and only time. A remarkable turn around which was duly celebrated in true Otter style in the pavilion at Cutler and later in the pavilion at Flitwick.

—

Dave Moules remembers Saturday 14th June 1969 the 1st XI travelled to the wonderfully named Nomansland Common to play Wheathampstead 1st XI. Flitwick batted first and scored a very respectable 196 for 8 before declaring. Top scorers were Dave Coleman (unluckily run out for 94), Bob Hartup (40) and yours truly with 23 including a six which was heading directly towards a lady sitting knitting in a deckchair by the boundary. Just as the ball seemed about to hit her she leant forward to study her knitting pattern on the grass at her feet. The ball passed over her head and smacked against the canvas of the deckchair, much to everyone's relief and especially hers when she realised how close she had come to serious harm. That was not the most memorable part of the day, however.

After tea Wheathampstead began their innings. Opening the batting was Carlton Franklin, a West Indian who, we were later to learn, was one of the players on stand-by in case of injuries to the touring West Indies side that summer. His opening partner was dismissed for 6 but the score was already past 50, as was Carlton F. Before hitting the ball he often had time to say 'Well bowled' or 'Good ball'. He did not call 'Yes', but stated how many runs he expected from the shot. So, 'Well bowled. Three' etc. was a recurring theme. He batted us into oblivion, rarely missing a ball, giving no chances and the result soon became a foregone conclusion. Wheathampstead reached 197 for the loss of 3 wickets in 40 overs (our innings lasted 47.5) with Carlton Franklin scoring 141 not out with 20 fours but no sixes. This was the most masterful piece of batting I ever witnessed outside of first-class cricket and from an unforgettable and gracious man to boot.

—

On Sunday 27th June 1976 Papworth 1st XI were visitors to the Rec to play a Millman Cup match. At that time Papworth were the top dogs of the league and one of the strongest sides in the Eastern area, with several current and ex-members of the Cambridgeshire Minor Counties side. Millman Cup rules stipulated that each innings should be of 45 overs with bowlers limited to 12 each. Points were awarded for a win with bonus batting and bowling points when certain targets were achieved.

Papworth batted first and had reached a massive 273 for 7 by the 40th over, all Flitwick's bowlers taking a bit of a hammering, especially from Vince Read who scored 86. The Papworth skipper decided to invoke (possibly for the first ever time) the Millman rule that allowed a side to declare short of the 45 overs and then have the overs not used added when they bowled.

This was a new experience for us and left us 50 overs to score 274 and them 50 to get us out and claim maximum points. Mick Shiner, an aggressive batsman, was sent in to open with

Andy Summerfield Snr but was soon out for 4. Andy and Keith Taylor kept the score ticking along with 70 and 44 respectively. Graham Wynn made 36 but the wheels began to wobble as 3 batsmen departed for only 15 runs between them. At 205 for 7, Mick Lee came to join me at the crease and the fun and games began. The ball was struck to all areas of the ground, suicidal quick singles, dashed twos and threes were taken and the target got closer. Finally, with 2 balls to spare, the score reached 275 for 7 and we had won, with Mick Lee (31 not out) and me (63 not out) virtually out on our feet. If ever there was a better run chase I'm glad I wasn't involved in it !

—

Richard Wigfield remembers a friendly match in July 1987 between Otters and Kodak, based in Hemel Hempstead. The traditional convoy of vehicles left The Vale on a hot summer's day and arrived at the venue to a friendly welcome from the opposition. However, there was a problem. The groundsman at the Kodak ground apparently had not been made aware that there was a game to be played that day, and no pitch had been prepared. Some discussions were held, including whether or not just to call it a draw and retire to the bar. However, as it was just a perfect day to play cricket, there was general agreement that every effort should be made to stage the game.

A set of keys were found to the groundsman's storage facility, and a team of dedicated players set about preparing a decent playing surface. All went well with the cutting and rolling of a strip, but then another challenge was faced. No whitewash to mark out the creases. After a short period of rummaging around, a solution was discovered in the guise of a tin of brilliant white gloss paint (non drip). After some further conversations about what the groundsman might think about the use of this paint, a decision was made that as he wasn't there and we would be long gone before he found out, the creases were duly marked with gloss paint and the game started. What then followed was the stuff of legends, but no names will be written here. Those concerned know who they are!

By this time, the paint had started to dry nicely, and the reflection off the creases from the bright sunshine just added to the normal difficulties faced by the batsman.

Flitwick batted first and amassed a total of 188 with contributions of 69 from Malcolm Wynn, 45 not out from Barry Payne and 28 from Les Ward. Tea was taken and Kodak took to the field in the afternoon sunshine. By now, the gloss paint had really started to set hard, and no re-marking of the lines was required.

Kodak's progress towards a winning total was steady, but they were always slightly behind the clock. The end of the game approached with Kodak requiring 25 runs required for victory. As the first couple of deliveries flew over the ropes for successive sixes, it was clear that the Kodak batsman had no intention whatsoever of giving this one up easily. A final total of 24 runs from the over was a magnificent effort, resulting in a tense and exciting draw with the scores level and the players returned to the bar for the then customary reflections on the game, and cricket in general.

The hospitality of our hosts was exemplary, and most of the Flitwick team were not shy in imbibing, but the witching hour approached, and it was decided that perhaps it would be best to head back to Bedfordshire. Well-oiled thanks and goodbyes were exchanged, and those Otters remaining headed outside to a car which had been very considerately driven round to the front of the Kodak pavilion to save weary legs. Upon attempting to move away, however, there was a rather disturbing noise from the front of the vehicle, and investigations realised that the car had actually been driven over a small wall outside the pavilion. Moving away was not an option, so a swift return to the bar was greeted with gusto, and further beverage consumption led to the agreement that several strong men would be required to lift the car off the wall. Volunteers obliged, and, eventually, goodbyes were said once again, and a group of weary Otters made their way home.

Rumours that the outlines of the creases can still be seen today are unconfirmed.

CLUB SONGS

In a past existence, I spent many hours sitting in a car travelling up and down motorways. Now I like driving, but it can be quite a lonely existence. To help pass the time, I thought how good it would be to have a club song that could be blasted out on appropriate (and perhaps sometimes inappropriate) occasions. You will no doubt have heard of the very successful West End show, *Joseph and his Amazing Technicolour Dreamcoat*. One line of one of the popular songs from the show was 'any dream will do' and to this day, I cannot remember what gave me the inspiration to change those words to 'any drink will do'.

From then on, the rest of the song was constructed as follows:

> *We're from The Vale,*
> *We're called The Otters (Woo oo woo)*
> *We play our cricket (Woo oo woo)*
> *In Bedfordshire.*
>
> *We like a drink*
> *Bitter or lager (Woo oo woo)*
> *Doesn't really matter (Woo oo woo)*
> *Any drink will do.*
> *A pint of best, a G&T*
>
> *Is good for you, is good for me,*
> *You can buy them, we will drink them*
> *Any drink will do.*

The song has been aired after victories, during social events (generally after a few drinks have been consumed), parties and at any other occasion where it was felt right to do so. After a few renditions, I decided that a series of actions should accompany the song and soon, the song could be performed with vocals, with vocals and actions, actions only then a final full rendition.

I then decided that of course, one was not enough. I took inspiration from the old time music hall favourite 'Daisy, Daisy, give me your answer do' as follows:

> *Flitwick, Flitwick, cricketers through and through.*
> *We're half crazy when we've had a drink or two.*
> *We may not be stylish batsmen (that's true)*
> *But when we've got our caps on.*
> *We look neat from our heads to our feet in our*
> *   colours of gold and blue.*

> *She was a sweet little dicky bird*
> *Tweet, tweet tweet, she went*
> *Softly she sang to me, 'til all our money was spent.*
> *Then she went away and we parted on fighting terms*
> *She was one of the early birds and I was one of the worms.*

This particular song has been heard usually after a famous victory or in the course of a raucous evening where many other songs, some far to near the knuckle to be re-produced on these pages, have been belted out.

This last song was one to which we were introduced at another cricket club, but one which has been sung on several occasions and venues. Perhaps the most famous venue and rendition was in a bar at Lord's at the national finals of the ECB indoor championships in 2011. The old ground had probably not seen or heard anything like it before.

It involves one individual standing on a stool or chair, starting the song. They then involve everyone else in the room, by pointing at random to the next person to stand on their stool at the end of each verse. The verse is sung again and each person standing on a stool then selects the next 'mountaineer'. Eventually the whole room is standing on a stool and can say they have been up sunshine mountain. The reverse journey then begins as the room comes down sunshine mountain.

As with many songs, the words have changed slightly over the course of time, but this is the original version.

We're going up the sunshine mountain, where the four
winds blow
We're going up the sunshine mountain, faces all aglow
Turn away from trouble and hold your head up high, Oh
We're going up the sunshine mountain, you and I.

For the reverse journey, simply replace *'we're going up the sunshine mountain'* with *'we're going down the sunshine mountain'*. The whole song can be completed with *'we've been up the sunshine mountain'*.

Now you must picture the movements involved.

During the first line, the 'mountaineers' march on the spot on their stool. At the end of the line, four puffs of wind are blown.

Second line, the marching on the spot continues with the back of the hands being tapped against the cheeks at the end of the line.

The third line is where the mayhem often occurs. The 'mountaineer' must turn a full circle. If they have selected a small bar stool, or perhaps one of dubious structural integrity, the occasional tumble has been known.

Final line, marching on the spot with the next victim being pointed at and the words 'you and I' being repeated, until all those currently on the mountain are satisfied that their selection has complied.

STATISTICS

The club has a very active web site and in 2011, the site was recorded as being the most active on the play cricket server, possibly as a result of the magnificent match reports that are produced after games, and an active forum for discussion including all things cricket, as well as the occasional 'favourite top 5' lists.

The labour of love entering the details of all the matches onto the club web site was carried out by several members, although Phil Gurney must be recognised for his efforts. His excellent match reports also are a source of continuing the recording of the club's playing history.

Much work has been put into populating the site with a plethora of statistics which those who wish to do so may peruse at their leisure. Rather than provide a list of statistics here, which by the time of publication will be out of date, why not visit the web site yourself and while away a few moments reminiscing about just how good you or your prodigies were/are.

http://flitwickcc.play-cricket.com

THE KIT BAG

A typical
1960s kit bag

PLAYING HISTORY AND THE TROPHY CABINET

- Joined the Hertfordshire League in 1998
- Eastern Counties League
- Millman Trophy
- Millman Competition
- Bedfordshire League (Founder Members)
- Joined the Home Counties League in 1984

- Bedfordshire County Premier League Winners 1997, 1998, 2010, 2012
- Bedfordshire County League Div 1 Winners 1992,1997
- Bedfordshire County League Div 4 Winners 2005
- Bedfordshire Indoor League 1 Winners 2005/6, 2006/7
- Bedfordshire Indoor Premier League Winners 2004/5, 2005/6, 2009/10
- Bedfordshire County League David Faill Fair Play Award 2008, 2010, 2012

- Christies Eastern Counties League 2nd XI Winners 1985,87,88

- Hertfordshire League Div 2 Winners 2010
- Hertfordshire League Div 2 Winners 1999
- Hertfordshire League Div 3 Winners 1998
- Hertfordshire League Div 7 Winners 2007
- Hertfordshire League Div 8 Winners 2001
- Hertfordshire League Div 9 Winners 1999
- Hertfordshire League Div 12 Winners 2012
- Hertfordshire League Div 11 Winners 2013

- Heritage Cup Winners 1995, 1996, 2007, 2012
- East Beds Shield Winners 1998

- Millman Trophy Div 3 3rd XI winners 2010
- Millman Trophy 2nd XI Winners Competition 1973

- Mid Beds Colts Cricket League U16 Winners 1986

- Beds Colts League Winners U11 2000
- Beds Colts League Winners U16 1991

- Beds Colts League South Winners U12 2007
- Beds Colts Indoor League Winners U13 2008
- Beds Colts League South Winners U10 2006
- Beds Colts League South Winners U12 2008
- Beds Colts League South Winners U14 2006, 2007
- Beds Colts League South Winners U16 2009

- Herts Knockout Cup Completion U13 winners 1985

- Luton Midweek League Division 4 Winners 1982
- Luton Midweek League Division 3 Winners 1984

- National Club Championship County Winners 2007

- Loo Seat Shield Flitwick 14 wins V Ampthill 6 wins
  Annual December Fixture

KEY MOMENTS IN FLITWICK'S HISTORY

1870 Flitwick Train Station opened.

1874 The Crown pub badly damaged by fire and looted by a drunken mob on Nov 5th.

1904 Flitwick Cricket Club formed.

1880 Roman coins dated about 270 A.D. found at Priestley farm.

1949 Flitwick Cricket Club re-formed after WWII.

1954 Redborne school opens.

1969 Flitwick village hall built.

1975 Decision taken to purchase new cricket ground.

1974
Woodland School opens.

1975
Flitwick Cricket Club featured in the first ever episode of *The Good Life*.

1978
Flitwick Cricket Club Clubhouse opens.

1977
First Flitwick carnival.

1981
Railway line electrified.

1981
First Cricket match played at The Vale.

1981
FCC v Northamptonshire CCC Peter Willey benefit match.

1983
First Flitwick Cricket Club tour.

1992

The Vale plays host to Radio 4's *Trivia Test Match* featuring Brian Johnstone, William Franklyn, Tim Rice, Willie Rushton & Paul Merton.

1993

3 sons born on July 2nd to 3 members of the Cricket club – Stefan Bodo (Michael), Richard Wigfield (John), Alistair Fuller (Jack) making national news.

2003

First Bedfordshire Senior County match played at The Vale.

1997

1stXI and 2ndXI are Bedfordshire Premier League and Division 1 Champions.

2007

Electronic scoreboard installed at The Vale.

2011

30 year anniversary game against Dunstable CC.

2014

A Bowled Move: A History of Flitwick Cricket Club is launched at The Hardy Vale.

2013

Ground re-named The Hardy Vale.